Healthy to 120 Version 2

Also available from Calworth Glenford

ENCYCLOPEDIA Of More Than 175 NATURAL HEALTH CURES - Volume 2 by Matt Cook

ENCYCLOPEDIA Of More Than 190 NATURAL HEALTH CURES - Volume 1 by Matt Cook

Healthy to 120 Version 1 by Matt Cook

Diabetes Formula for Life by Matt Cook

Oxygen Remedy by Richard Geller

Endless Honeymoon by Matt Cook

Fix Your Digestion — Fix Your Life by Matt Cook

Forever Wealthy Without Stocks and Bonds by Richard Geller

Great Writing Wins Cases by Naomi Scheck

How to Raise Money to Start and Expand Your Business by Richard Geller

Make a Fortune Settling Other People's Debts by Richard Geller

Prostate Rewind by Matt Cook

Mortgage Relief Formula by Richard Geller

Wealthy Family Secrets by Richard Geller

Healthy to 120 Version 2

Surviving and Thriving
Despite Modern Medicine

By Matt Cook

Calworth Glenford LLC
1005 Country Club Avenue
Cheyenne, Wyoming 82001 USA

Managing Editor: Richard Geller
Cover Design: Fred C. DeLong
Production and Printing: Grosvenor Publications Limited

ISBN-13: 978-0-9995040-1-7

Printed in the United States of America

Highlights

❖ Modern medicines and our poisonous food chain are more likely to kill you than old age.

❖ Intestinal inflammation is the culprit causing the symptoms that modern medicines merely mask. But, worse yet, these strong "medicines" create even more profound health risks.

❖ How giant and greedy pharmaceutical companies are after your wallet while caring little or nothing about your health.

❖ What you need to begin doing RIGHT NOW to regain your health and enjoy an active and vigorous sex life well into old, old age!

Table of Contents

The List of Serious Medical Issues We've Been Misguided About Goes On and On

To Live Long — Avoid Doctors

Today's society has a strong but misplaced belief that modern medicine will cure almost everything that ails anyone. Many people think a permanent cure for all types of cancer is only one engineered gene away. Our modern society expects instant gratification and we believe that having a few pills prescribed by a doctor will make everything better in a day or two.

Rosario Schielzeth lived to the age of 104. As is customary on every birthday of a centenarian, Rosario was asked what she attributed her long life to. She had two short answers to that question:

1. Watch what you eat.

2. Stay away from doctors.

Rosario was just an ordinary woman who figured out how to live a long healthy life. She was not a member of a hidden jungle tribe that had never been exposed to modern medicine. Rosario was from Florida. She enjoyed good eyesight, good hearing, and good mobility, though she did use a walker to get around. Until her final day, she continued going to the movies, the mall, and the beach for ice cream. Another amazing thing about Ms. Schielzeth is that she was the round-the-clock caretaker for her 87-year-old daughter, an Alzheimer's patient.

Fred Kummerow lived to age 102. Not bad for a man born in Berlin, Germany in 1914 at the beginning of World War I. Despite enormous challenges in life, he reported that at age 100 he was enjoying much of the best time of his life. Fred is a contrast to Rosario because Fred was a scientist who fought the food industry and prevailing medical practices for decades until his early warnings about the dangers of trans fats (PUFAs) were finally vindicated. He maintained a research laboratory until he was 101. He also had an interest in the study of nutrition, dating to his days as a student, when he had to care for laboratory rats. Fred published his first scientific paper in 1957 challenging the food industry about the dangers of PUFAs. In Fred's words, these are "a diet of sudden death."

He reported his findings in hundreds of papers, but his research was ignored and disparaged for years. Still, his ideas slowly caught on with other scientists, but the Food and Drug Administration made no official recommendation. In 2009, he demanded a formal response from the FDA. Although federal law requires a response within 180 days, Fred had to sue the FDA in 2013 (at age 98). He was granted a "tentative determination" that PUFAs are not safe for human consumption but it was not until 2015 that the FDA formally declared that PUFAs should be eliminated from the U.S. food supply by 2018. But don't be fooled by that declaration. PUFAs still thrive in our food chain and remain the killer that scientist Fred Kummerow knew them to be from the beginning. Fred Kummerow is one of the great public health heroes of our times. Into his 100s, he ate eggs and cheese, and drank whole milk. He avoided french fries, margarine, and other fried foods. At his 100th birthday party, he even passed on the store-bought cake someone brought after he noticed it contained trans fat.

Your love life can prevail. In December of 2019, Charlotte and John Henderson celebrated 80 years of marriage at the ages of 105 and 106 respectfully. According to Guinness World Records, they are the oldest living couple on earth. John remembers hearing his first radio broadcast in 1912. Both had long careers and began their Golden Years when John retired in 1972 (during Watergate). In retirement, they occupied themselves with travel — mostly cruises. They have sailed around South America, Scandinavia, China, and dozens of other locales. John is the oldest living former football player for the University of Texas. They have attended at least one UT game per season for the past 84 years. Attending games became easier in the past ten years after they returned to live in Austin. So, what's the couple's secret to their longevity? Living in moderation, they said. They eat right, don't drink much, and John still exercises at the community gym almost every day. Except for some hearing loss, both are in excellent health!

Medical Disclaimer

I am not a doctor, nor do I play one on TV. So I am not qualified to give anyone medical advice. I am simply sharing the knowledge that I have acquired through extensive research about the best ways to remain healthy, live a robust life into old age, and maintain the sexual health that so many men lose as they age. Before embracing any of the suggestions you read in this book, it is **vitally important that you consult with your doctor or health care provider**. I strongly recommend that, after reading this book, you have an open and completely honest conversation with your doctor about how you may or may not want to change your current treatments. If you are not satisfied with your doctor's advice after that conversation, you could consult with another doctor. But under no circumstances should you alter your treatment without the agreement and on-going care of a doctor knowledgeable about you and your health.

Death by Drugs

Death by medicine is a 21st-century epidemic. When you consider that **prescription drugs are now killing far more people than illegal drugs**, it is clear that America's "War on Drugs" is directed at the wrong enemy.

The most commonly abused prescription drugs are OxyContin, Vicodin, Xanax, and Soma, and they now cause more deaths than heroin and cocaine combined. In fact, prescription drugs are now the preferred "high" for many, especially teens, as they are typically used legally, which eliminates the stigma of being labeled a junkie.

But in fact, these prescription drugs are now the drugs of choice among the addict crowd, and they are highly profitable on the black market. Importantly, **many over-the-counter drugs that are not opiates are just as dangerous to your health and ultimately to your life.**

These are the modern "miracle" drugs that are used to treat a myriad of diseases that are presumed to be life-threatening, such as diabetes, high blood pressure, prostate concerns, heart disease, a wide variety of cancers, and many other diseases that may or may not even exist.

Ask yourself this question: Why is that that every month or so the pharmaceutical companies come out with a new drug to cure a disease or health condition that nobody had heard of until the new drug is unveiled? Could it be there is no such disease, but that Big Pharma needs to create a new market for a new concoction?

Americans Are Drug Crazed

According to an article in *Mail Online:*

> *"Americans consume 80% of the world's supply of painkillers — more than 110 tons of pure, addictive opiates every year — as the country's prescription drug abuse epidemic explodes. That's enough drugs to give every single American 64 Percocets or Vicodin. And pain pill prescriptions continue to surge, up 600 % in 10 years, thanks to doctors who are more and more willing to hand out drugs to patients who are suffering."*

Conflicts of Interest Encourage Some Drugs

This is merely one small example of how big pharma exercises their clout. Under Florida's 2012 PIP (personal injury protection) reform law, Floridians will no longer be able to seek massage therapy or acupuncture treatments after a car accident, as these services will no longer be covered under Florida PIP insurance. The primary treatment option left for those who suffer from pain as a result of a car accident is — you guessed it — pain killers! This is despite the fact that the most common injury caused by auto accidents is soft tissue damage, which is ideally treated through massage, not pain killers that can potentially compound your misery with addiction and liver damage.

Avoiding Doctors

The best strategy for achieving health is avoiding a visit to your doctor in the first place. Why? Because in many cases you will simply leave the doctor's office with a prescription or two which probably won't even solve your health problem. Most doctor visits result in "solutions" that only suppress your symptoms, while causing other side effects and problems.

Rather than advising patients about the true underlying conditions and real solutions that can lead to better health, doctors often resort to toxic Band-Aid solutions. There are actually many reasons why avoiding your doctor may be in the best interest of your health.

Cholesterol. Many doctors are unaware that a high-fat diet is NOT the cause of heart disease. They have been fooled into believing that total cholesterol is an accurate predictor of heart health. If you visit your physician and you have high cholesterol, you're likely to be told two things:

1. Take a statin cholesterol-lowering drug, and

2. Don't eat saturated fats.

While statin drugs do lower cholesterol very effectively, **cholesterol is not the culprit in heart disease**. A report by the Massachusetts Institute of Technology concluded that **no study has ever**

7

ns increase your life expectancy.
tins does not prolong your life at
roving your life, they actually
rioration in the quality of your
...g muscles, endangering your liver
and kidneys, and even compromising heart
function. Even worse, statins cause type 2 diabetes,
ED, and are linked to ALS-like symptoms.

The best ways to optimize your cholesterol levels
and your heart health involve diet and lifestyle
choices, including eating healthy minimally-
processed fats and avoiding highly-processed
vegetable fats and oils that are loaded with toxic
omega-6 fatty acids.

Depression. People often leave a doctor's or
psychiatrist's office with a prescription that causes
more health problems than it solves. In a typical
year, 230 million prescriptions are written for
antidepressants. Many studies have been conducted
on this. Overwhelmingly, independent studies (not
involving pharmaceutical companies) show about
50% of patients receiving antidepressant
medications show improvement while 30% of those
receiving a placebo also show improvement. One
important question to ask is: How many of those
receiving the antidepressant medications are
experiencing the same cause for improvement as
those taking a placebo?

Still, one out of every 20 patients reports that th
remain depressed. Of these, 80% report some level
of functional impairment at work, in daily living,
and in getting along with other people.

With these drugs so extensively prescribed, why are
so many people still feeling low? The psychiatric
industry brings in an estimated $330 billion
annually. That's a mighty good income for an
industry that offers little in the way of actual
cures.

Research confirms that such medications are no
more effective than sugar pills. Some medical
professionals now think this is due to a placebo
effect where receiving either pill suggests to the
patient that a cure is at hand — miraculously the
patient cures him or herself! In fact, due to harmful
side effects, the real pills are dangerous while the
sugar pills are not!

The side effects of potent antidepressant drugs can
be deadly. Each year, approximately 750,000
Americans attempt suicide and 30,000 succeed.
There is no solid proof that taking these drugs
relieves any symptoms, but they may increase the
chance that people will try to kill themselves.

Better choices include natural remedies such as
exercise, the Emotional Freedom Technique,
vitamin D, and proper nutrition. None of these
contribute to the balance sheets of pharmaceutical

ᴖ

· doctors. Therefore, they are mostly ainstream medicine.

...gh blood pressure. In 2003, the Joint National Committee on Prevention, Detection, Evaluation and Treatment of High Blood Pressure (an organization rife with drug industry conflicts of interest) decided that what were previously considered relatively low blood pressure readings suddenly constituted a risk for heart disease. **Further lowering the blood pressure threshold to 140/90 enabled the drug companies to peddle high blood pressure medicine (loaded with side effects) to an additional 45 million Americans.**

But that only fueled the discussion within the research community, many of whom argue that decreasing the lower threshold has exposed more people to dangerous side effects without reliable proof of health benefits. In 2014, the Eighth Joint National Committee (JNC8) said that adults aged 60 or older should only take blood pressure medication if their blood pressure exceeds 150/90, a higher bar of treatment than the 2003 guideline of 140/90.

The JNC8 recommendations were based on clinical trials that proved that stricter guidelines and tighter blood pressure control provided no additional benefit to patients.

The JNC8 recommendation is that people with borderline high blood pressure (stoic pressure

between 140 and 149) resort to more natural control remedies, such as implementing a healthy nutrition plan, exercising, and using effective stress reduction techniques that will normalize blood pressure for most people.

PSA Test for Prostate Cancer is Worthless

The prostate-specific antigen test (PSA test) is unreliable at best and often leads to unnecessary treatments that can cause complications and undermine health. A positive PSA reading is interpreted as indicating cancer, but can actually be caused by an enlarged or infected prostate. The suspicion of cancer leads to a biopsy and that can cause a serious or even deadly infection.

The PSA test has little or no effect on mortality outcomes and is NOT recommended.

Prostate cancers are unusual cancers. Most prostate cancers grow very slowly without causing any noticeable symptoms or problems. These cancers include:

❖ **Adenocarcinoma** is the most common type of prostate cancer. Over 95% of prostate cancers are this type. Adenocarcinoma is slow-growing and, though it often remains organ-contained, it does have the potential to spread to other parts of the body, such as the lymph nodes, bones, and other organs.

❖ **Small cell carcinoma** is a rare aggressive prostate cancer that initially forms in specialized cells within the prostate. This form of prostate cancer usually doesn't affect the PSA level and is difficult to diagnose.

❖ There are other very rare forms of prostate cancer that are also difficult to diagnose.

Prostate cancer is unusual among cancers because many tumors never spread from the prostate. Even if it does spread, prostate cancer is often easy to treat and men go on to live in good health for many years. Indications that it is spreading include pain, fatigue, and other symptoms.

Many experts agree that PSA testing is unreliable at best and useless at worst for accurately diagnosing prostate cancer. It is also widely recognized that routine PSA blood tests often lead to over-diagnosis of prostate cancer resulting in unnecessary treatments.

Like mammograms, the PSA screen has become little more than an up-selling technique. The false positive rate is high, and the bulk of the harm results from subsequent unnecessary treatments. But it is a moneymaker for doctors and Big Pharma!

You can improve your chances of avoiding prostate cancer by including plenty of certain vegetables and some animal proteins in your diet and minimizing your use of tobacco. However, it is even more important to avoid internal inflammation and estrogens.

You don't need to limit carbohydrates such as sugar/fructose.

However, highly processed or charcoaled meats, whole grains (yes, whole grains), synthetic trans-fats, and especially PUFA fats are associated with an increased risk for prostate cancer and should be avoided.

Dietary Recommendations Have Changed

Most doctors are clueless about what constitutes a healthy diet. They recommend such health disasters as artificial sweeteners instead of natural sugars, vegetable oils in lieu of butter, and fat-free pasteurized dairy products. Most will also neglect to tell you about the foods you should be eating more of to optimize your health, including well-cooked vegetables, dairy products from grass-fed cattle, healthy saturated fats from grass-fed beef, and more.

Quite honestly, I don't recommend the advice in the report published jointly every five years (most recently 2020) by the US Department of Health and Human Services (HHS) and the US Department of Agriculture (USDA). This report is supposed to provide the public with nutritional and dietary information and guidelines, but it's fraught with political agendas and puts too much reliance on studies that are outdated. Yet, this is the report that's most relied on by major organizations, such as the American Heart Association, the American Diabetes Association, federal school lunch programs, and many others.

Because nutritionists are on the forefront of all of the latest nutrition knowledge, they're constantly updating their own diets based on the most current research. Rather than putting blind faith in doctors, you can learn a lot more by talking to nutrition experts about how their daily diets have changed over the past five years as they monitor emerging science.

Elisa Zied, MS, RDN, CDN tells us: *"Although I don't subscribe to fasting or suggest going more than three or four waking hours without food, my diet has evolved into one in which I consume most of my calories during the day. I always start my morning with one large or two small breakfasts, and I almost always have a big lunch. And instead of a traditional dinner, I'll choose one or two small snacks. I find that I feel more energized when I eat this way and it also allows me to fit in more food groups and maintain a healthy weight."*

Lisa Moskovitz, RD, CDN says: *"Over the past five years, I've focused a lot on eating more whole foods and less processed ones. Processed foods, which are those that have been altered so they're no longer in their most natural state, usually contain a ton of additives, blood-sugar spiking sugar, and chemicals that don't offer many advantages for your health."*

Lisa goes on to say: *'Recently, full-fat dairy has come back into my diet. Not only does it taste much better than reduced-fat alternatives, but it keeps me far more satisfied and helps with vitamin D absorption."*

Alissa Rumsey, spokesperson for the Academy of Nutrition and Dietetics, has also changed her diet to include more healthy fats: *'Five years ago, I was using skim milk in my coffee, eating 0% fat yogurts, and choosing low-fat cottage cheese. Now I use whole milk in my coffee and choose 2% or 4% Greek yogurt and cottage cheese."*

Registered dietitians Lauren Slayton and Torey Armul are also on board with the full-fat trend, incorporating things like a moderate amount of uncooked olive oil (teaspoon per day), fish, butter, ghee, and coconut oil into their daily diets. "Fat is the only macronutrient that doesn't raise your blood sugar. In a typical day I'll have a good fat at every meal," Slayton tells us.

While I don't completely agree with every recommendation these dietitians make, I do think they are much more forward-thinking than the doctors who haven't reviewed dietary recommendations since their first year of pre-med.

Personally, I don't normally have a large breakfast. Usually, I start my day with a glass of milk and an egg or two. If you want more, I suggest including some cheese and/or a tortilla. A glass of orange juice is always good and healthy. You might also want to add some collagen to a glass of milk for lunch and snack on cheese during the day. I eat a small dinner that includes some carbohydrates and protein. Generally, I eat throughout the day instead of one or two large meals.

For a short time, I thought olive oil was better for you than it is. The benefit of olive oil is that it is not filtered and not cooked (it should not be used for cooking). However, further research showed it has more PUFAs than originally thought. Unfortunately, olive oil has caught on as a fad with too many people continuing to recommend it. I suggest using it in a limited amount (always uncooked and no more than one teaspoon a day) as a flavoring on salads and vegetables.

Is Your Doctor Telling the Truth?

Most Americans (79% according to a survey) implicitly trust their doctors. However, a survey of

1,900 physicians revealed that not all doctors are always completely honest with patients. The results of that study showed that:

❖ One-third of physicians did not completely agree with disclosing serious medical errors to patients.

❖ One-fifth did not completely agree that physicians should never tell a patient something untrue.

❖ Amazingly, 40% believed that they should <u>hide their financial relationships with drug and device companies</u> from their patients.

❖ 10% said they had told patients something untrue in the previous year.

Medical Disclaimer #2

It's your health we're talking about here and without your health, you have nothing. I would never try to dissuade you from consulting with a doctor before making potentially life-changing decisions. Hopefully, you have chosen a health care provider whose expertise you trust and whose philosophies about health are similar to your own. However, if you have been following their advice for a while and are not experiencing the results that you desire or were told you to expect, you may want to consider another opinion.

It's important to ask questions before opting for tests, procedures, or treatments, and it's your decision if you'd rather opt for less medical intervention while choosing a more natural way of healing your body.

Ultimately, the more you take responsibility for your own health (in the form of nurturing your body to prevent disease), and the less you rely on the "disease care" that passes for health care, the better. If you carefully abide by some basic health principles — simple things like staying active, eating whole foods, sleeping enough, getting sun exposure, reducing stress in your life, and nurturing personal relationships — you will drastically reduce your need for conventional medical care. This in and of itself will reduce your chances of suffering negative side effects.

In the event you do need medical care, seek a health care practitioner who will help you move toward complete wellness by helping you discover and understand the hidden causes of your health challenges. Instead of following a one-size-fits-all health plan, you need to create a customized, comprehensive, and holistic treatment plan for you.

What Long-Lived People Do

As much-touted as the health care systems of the US and other first world countries are (Canada, Great Britain, Germany, etc.), you'd expect these countries to be at the top of the list of nations where significant numbers of people live to a ripe old age. But you would be wrong!

The populations who tend to live well into old age also tend to be in relatively remote locations and relatively disconnected from modern society. In general, these people get their food from the land. You won't find boxed foods from grocery stores in their pantries.

The Five Places with the Longest-Living Populations

The National Geographic Society lists the five top places for longevity:

❖ **Okinawa, Japan** is an archipelago 360 miles off the coast of Japan and that's where you'll find the highest prevalence of proven centenarians in the world: 740 out of a population of 1.3 million. Okinawan seniors not only have the longest life expectancy in the world, but also the best health expectancy — they remain vigorous and healthy into old age, suffering relatively few age-related ailments.

One of their secrets is gardening, which provides a moderate amount of exercise, exposure to sunlight, and nutritious food. Another Okinawan habit is to obey an old adage that says, " eat until you are 80% full," instead of gorging. They also have a sense of purpose, a positive outlook on life, and close social support groups.

❖ **Sardinia, Italy** is an island 120 miles off the coast of Italy where the men — mostly farmers and shepherds — are particularly long-lived. In fact, one town of 1,700 people, Ovodda, boasts five centenarians.

Their secrets to longevity include eating a healthy Mediterranean diet and consuming lots of goat cheese and goat milk. They walk a lot, they also take time for leisure, and they maintain a positive attitude and sense of humor about life.

❖ **Loma Linda, California** is the single U.S. location on the list, but the people who live there have a non-standard lifestyle. East of Los Angeles, Loma Linda is a community that includes about 9,000 Seventh-Day Adventists, a religious group whose members are significantly longer-lived than the average American. Adventist culture focuses on healthful habits such as vegetarianism and warns against alcohol and smoking.

Their secrets to longevity include healthful habits that are integral to their belief system. Adventists drink plenty of water, eat lots of nuts, exercise lightly on a regular basis, and tend to maintain a healthy weight. They nurture emotional and spiritual health, value their family relationships, and prize volunteering.

❖ **Nicoya, Costa Rica** is an inland community situated on the remote Nicoya peninsula. Middle-age mortality among the community is remarkably low: A man at age 60 has about twice the chance of reaching age 90 than a man of the same age living in the U.S. The community also has the lowest rates of cancer in Costa Rica.

Their secret to longevity is a sense of purpose in life that fosters a physically active lifestyle. They spend plenty of time outdoors and on family and spirituality. They also sleep eight hours a night and their diet includes nutrient-rich foods and water that's naturally high in calcium and magnesium.

❖ **Ikaria, Greece** is a Greek island 35 miles off the coast of Turkey. Like Nicoya, the population includes many nonagenarians — people there are three times more likely to reach the age of 90 than Americans are. According to the Blue Zones website: "Chronic diseases are a rarity in Ikaria. People living in this region have 20% less cancer, half the rate of cardiovascular disease and almost no dementia!"

One of their secrets to longevity is a mineral hot springs — Ikaria has been a health destination for centuries. Residents stay active through walking, farming, and fishing, but they also make sure to take time out to nap and socialize. In addition to their Mediterranean diet, they eat a lot of wild greens and drink an herbal tea that's full of nutrients. Their community lifestyle encourages good health habits and regular social engagement.

What These Cultures Have In Common

Researcher Dan Buettner, who studies these populations for the National Geographic Society, calls these long-lived pockets "Blue Zones". Though the top five Blue Zones are relatively isolated and scattered around the globe, here's what they have in common, according to the *New York Times*:

❖ A cultural environment that reinforces healthy lifestyle habits like exercise and a healthy diet.

❖ Healthy social relationships and psychological well-being.

❖ People who have a cooperative spirit.

❖ People who tend gardens.

❖ Public health that is easily accessible.

❖ Seniors are valued as members of their families and the community.

Another common trait among the longest-lived societies is they consume little or no refined sugars (but plenty of fruit sugar) and other processed foods. But this is changing with increased globalization — diets are becoming more Americanized in all of these once-remote places. This is already having an adverse effect on the health and longevity of the people in these communities.

No Workouts
Of course, you don't have to be a member of one of these long-living populations to have a long life yourself. Maintaining a daily routine that is similar to theirs will go a long way toward helping you live a long and healthy life.

But do you want to start an exercise routine involving a new wardrobe of workout clothes, a gym membership, dedicating several hours every week

23

to becoming a gym rat, showering twice a day, and having to commute to the gym regularly?

Well, the good news is that you don't have to do any of that. BUT, you do need to make some crucial lifestyle changes so that your lifestyle is more active and blends perfectly into your current daily routine.

Regardless of your age, gender, race (or any other factor that defines who you are), you can become more active. You can do things that you enjoy and even use these activities as playtime. Something as simple as a gentle game of tag with the grandkids will do wonders for your health.

Do you have a swimming pool in your back yard that you haven't been in for years? You don't need commit to the chore of 50 daily laps. Just get out there and frolic once in a while. You'll quickly feel years younger just as a result of playing.

What do you do when you feel a bit stressed? Do you head for the refrigerator as many people do? Why not take a 15-minute walk around the neighborhood instead? You will meet your neighbors and maybe get in on another play activity like horseshoes. Or find a new golf partner.

Go on a picnic, go fly a kite, go to the beach for the day. Go on vacation and actually get out of the hotel to see the sights. Or check out the sights in your own town. It's surprising how many people never visit the sights that are just beyond their own back yards.

What about volunteering? It doesn't take much effort to hand out groceries to the less fortunate once a week. That is guaranteed to put a smile on your face while you get to meet new people.

Clean your house or wash your car. Do you really need a housekeeper to do your chores once a week while you sit in front of the TV? You can get into better shape (and enjoy a clean house) just by dusting, vacuuming, and mopping once or twice a week.

And that automated car wash is just another activity thief. Back in your father's day (maybe your grandfather's day), people took huge pride in their cars. They washed them by hand once or twice a month to keep them looking spiffy.

When you're at the office, take a break once in a while. Walk to the bathroom. Go visit your colleagues' offices to say hi. A *European Heart Journal* study of 5,000 men and women found that the 25% of participants who took the most breaks during the workday were 1.6 inches thinner than the quarter who took the fewest breaks.

Even if watching TV is one of your favorite pastimes, you can still be more active. Stash the remote somewhere and get up to change the channel. During commercials, stretching will give you an instant jolt of energy and will help you straighten your back and ease that nasty back pain.

Now, you might be thinking that stretching won't be of much help. You don't know that until you try it! It could be the perfect way for you to begin enjoying more daily activities on your way to better health.

Adding one or two activities to your daily routine can make the difference between a long and healthy life and a life fraught with disease and doctors. Avoid doctors.

**You have the power to change your life.
You can change your lifestyle to one that is healthier.**

Social Networks

Maybe it's a bowling league, shooting hoops with friends once a week, dance lessons, or a bingo parlor. Those are all social networks for adults that can be found in most communities. And most of them increase the activity levels of adults when they most need it.

Today, the term "social network" makes most of us

think of websites like Facebook. Though these are great tools for staying in touch with family and friends who don't live nearby, all of us really need face-to-face meetings where personalities come through fully and some physical contact is involved.

Social support is important to both your physical and mental health. Too many people spend much of their time in isolation and loneliness rather than with companions. Yes, lack of social support really can hinder a person's overall quality of life.

As people age, they develop well-entrenched routines. Getting up each day to the same breakfast, the same TV programs, and washing the same three plates and four glasses in the sink at the end of each day can literally cause people to lose track of what day of the week it is and the date of the month. They might not even remember who the president is. Lack of social support is related to negative impacts on health and wellbeing, especially for older people.

Having a variety of positive social supports contributes to the psychological and physical wellness of elderly individuals. Support from others can be an important factor in reducing stress, improving physical health, and defeating psychological problems such as depression and anxiety. But people (not doctors) are required.

The need for community-based services is more important now than ever before. Isolated people can find the support they need in many places including senior centers, assisted living facilities, meal delivery programs, religious affiliations, adult day care centers, and more.

Community-based services can be extremely important for elderly individuals. Services for older persons can encompass many aspects of life, but one of the most important is the social support they offer. This positive social support can help older persons defeat loneliness and isolation.

However, to be effective, social support must involve more than just physical presence or conversation. Studies have shown that social support services should include quality activities, and these activities should promote positive self-awareness.

Self-awareness is one key to maintaining mental health as we age. People who maintain self-awareness also tend to take better care of themselves physically. While sports and other athletic activities work well for younger people, these are not always appropriate for the elderly. You're not going to find many 85 year olds on the basketball court — but you will probably find some taking dance lessons.

Activities that are more appropriate for elderly individuals include reminiscence groups, joint journal writing, readings of favorite book passages, group exercise, singing groups, etc. Individuals may also feel more self-satisfied if they are involved in the planning of such social activities.

Today, there are more than 15,000 senior centers and adult care centers across the US. Senior centers act as a focal point where older Americans can receive many aging services, including physical activities that help keep them vibrant.

The most common services offered at senior centers include health programs (including Zumba and Yoga), arts/humanities activities, intergenerational programs, employment assistance, community action opportunities, transportation services, volunteer opportunities, education opportunities, financial assistance, senior rights counseling/legal services, travel programs, and meal programs. All of these programs and activities foster positive self-awareness.

At the crux of it is networking with others. Adult day care programs provide social support and health services to older adults during the daytime. Most centers operate Monday through Friday during normal business hours. They provide meals and health services, but a major way they differ from other programs for the elderly is that they help participants develop and increase self-awareness by encouraging independence.

They also offer social support services such as musical entertainment and singing groups, group games such as cards, gentle exercise, discussion groups, holiday/birthday celebrations, and local outings.

In addition to enjoying the social activities provided, participants of such programs may also develop lasting relationships with staff and other participants.

Living to a quality ripe old age doesn't only require avoiding doctors and strong medicines. It's also important to **enjoy a self-fulfilling life with plenty of activity and people in it.**

Avoiding the #1 Killer

Would you be surprised if I told you that **STRESS is the number one killer**? Well, it is.

How does stress kill?

Stress in and of itself isn't a killer. What kills are its **negative effects on the body**. A few of the more serious health problems can be brought on by the effects of stress are high blood pressure, heart attacks, anxiety, and depression. Stress causes certain hormones to get out of whack. Chronic activation of those hormones can cause damage to our brains and vasculature (the arrangement of blood vessels in the body or within an organ).

Stress causes a spike in inflammatory cytokines. Inflammatory cytokines are chemicals released by the immune system, which activate armies of cells to attack invaders such as viruses, pathogenic bacteria, and cancer cells.

That is supposed to be a defense, a good thing. But the immune system can be over-activated, which can lead to autoimmune disease. Most modern chronic diseases — including atherosclerosis, depressive disorders, and other diseases that linger and are difficult to treat and conquer — are associated with elevated levels of these cytokines and elevations in autoimmunity. This connection is confirmed by many studies that demonstrate a link

31

between a history of trauma (of all sorts) and elevations in cytokines.

Stress as Defined by Hans Selye

Stress as we currently understand it was first defined by Hans Selye in 1936 as "the non-specific response of the body to any demand for change".

Selye noted in numerous experiments that laboratory animals subjected to acute but different noxious physical and emotional stimuli (blaring light, deafening noise, extremes of heat or cold, perpetual frustration) all exhibited the same pathologic changes: stomach ulcerations, shrinkage of lymphoid tissue, and enlargement of the adrenals.

He later demonstrated that persistent stress could cause these animals to develop a variety of diseases similar to those that afflict humans, including heart attack, stroke, kidney disease, and rheumatoid arthritis.

Stress can increase productivity — but only up to a point. Once that point is reached, things go downhill rapidly. Selye struggled unsuccessfully throughout his life to find a satisfactory definition for stress. In attempting to extrapolate his animal studies to humans so that people would understand what he meant, he redefined stress as **"The rate of wear and tear on the body"**. This is actually a pretty good description of biological aging, so it is not surprising that increased stress can accelerate many aspects of the aging process.

Stress Is Like a Roller Coaster

Stress is difficult to define because its effects are different for each of us. A good example of this would be studying riders on a steep roller coaster.

At the back of the roller coaster are the people who hunch down in their seats with their eyes shut, their jaws clenched, and a white-knuckled grip on the retaining bar. They can't wait for the ride in the torture device to be over so they can get back on solid ground and get away.

Up front are the thrill-seekers, wide-eyed, yelling with excitement, and relishing each steep plunge. When the ride is over, they are first in line to get on the very next ride.

In between, you may see a few riders who are bored to the point of nonchalance.

So, was the roller coaster ride stressful or not?

Stress Hormones

Here we will discuss four specific hormones that cause stress:

❖ Estrogen

❖ Cortisol

❖ Serotonin

❖ Histamine

Stress Caused by Estrogen

Research conducted by scientists at Yale University showed that high levels of the female sex hormone estrogen affect the brain's ability to cope with stress. Estrogen was found to amplify the stress response in areas of the brain most closely associated with depression and other stress-related mental illnesses. Researchers say the findings may one-day lead to the development of reliable treatments for depression.

Essentially, there are two ways that excess estrogen accumulates in the body. **The body can produce too much estrogen or it can absorb it from the environment.** You can make an effort to stick to a diet that helps limit the amount of estrogen your body produces.

Unfortunately, in our culture we are exposed to estrogen in many ways. For example, there are estrogen-like compounds in some foods. The toxic pesticides, herbicides, and growth hormones in our food supply are full of estrogen promoters.

Pharmaceutical hormones, such as those used in hormone-replacement therapy (HRT), can also increase our exposure to estrogen — whether we take them actively or absorb them after they've made their way into our drinking water.

We are living in a virtual sea of harmful estrogens, and researchers are only now beginning to identify the extent of harm this is causing to human health.

Mitigating our exposure to estrogen requires healthy life choices, and that can't be achieved by taking even more strong medications. What it does require is that we are careful about what we eat and don't eat. Take care of your liver (limit alcohol consumption), don't use drugs, and maintain a healthy weight.

We'll get into more details about this later, but you also need to include healthy bacteria in your diet. This improves your digestion, eliminates gut inflammation, and **improves your body's ability to remove estrogen through the digestive tract.** You're might want to include a daily probiotic in your daily diet.

As I mentioned above, pesticides, herbicides, and growth hormones encourage the proliferation of estrogen in your body. One healthy lifestyle choice you can make to reduce your exposure to excess estrogen is to choose organic dairy products and grass-fed meats.

There are nutrients that, if ingested in sufficient quantity, will support the body's ability to break down and eliminate estrogen. These include zinc, magnesium, and vitamin B6 (among others).

Avoid exposure to xenoestrogens — these are in plastics, cosmetics, and many, many common consumer products. Xenoestrogens mimic the effects of estrogens.

And who would think you'd need to be cautious about soy? Well, soy naturally contains a relatively high concentration of some types of estrogens, so avoid soy products like tofu and soymilk (soy sauce is fine).

Sleep well. Poor sleep hygiene causes a reduction in melatonin, a hormone that helps protect against estrogen dominance. Aim for seven to eight hours of sleep per night in a cool, dark room.

As the body responds to high levels of stress, it "steals" progesterone to manufacture the stress hormone cortisol, which often results in an excess of estrogen, which amplifies the stress response in the brain. What a vicious cycle.

Cortisol — the Stress Hormone

The stress hormone cortisol is public health enemy number one. Scientists have known for years that elevated cortisol levels interfere with learning and memory. They also contribute to suppression of immune function, lower bone density, weight gain, and increases in blood pressure, cholesterol, and heart disease... the list goes on and on.

Cortisol causes a lot of health problems with one that is particularly important to men. Testosterone and cortisol have opposite effects on men's health (including sex health). Cortisol works against the youthful and masculinizing effects of testosterone in a number of ways. Men with belly fat, low sex drive, erection problems, diabetes, etc. often have chronically high cortisol and therefore very low testosterone. Anything that sends testosterone levels up and cortisol levels down at the same time has a high probability of being beneficial for most men.

Chronic stress and elevated cortisol levels also increase your risk for depression, mental illness, and **lower life expectancy**. Cortisol is released by the adrenal glands in response to fear or stress as part of the fight-or-flight mechanism. The fight-or-flight mechanism is an aspect of the general adaptation syndrome defined in 1936 by biochemist Hans Selye.

Below are 5 everyday tips to help you reduce your cortisol levels:

1. **Regular physical activity** such as walking, jogging, swimming, biking, and riding the

elliptical... these are great ways to activate the "flight" outlet to burn up cortisol. A little bit of cardio goes a long way. Just 20 to 30 minutes of activity most days of the week pays huge dividends by lowering cortisol every day and for the long run.

2. **Meditation reduces anxiety and lowers cortisol levels.** The simple act of relaxing engages the vagus nerve which in turn triggers a signal within your nervous system to slow your heart rate, lower your blood pressure, and decrease your cortisol levels. The next time you find yourself in a stressful situation, meditate for a moment until you decompress and feel your entire body relax.

There are many different types of meditation. "Meditating" doesn't have to be a sacred or New Age mind-bending experience. Do some research, visit a meditation center if you can, and fine-tune a daily meditation practice that fits your schedule and personality.

Setting aside 10 to 15 minutes to practice mindfulness or meditation fosters a sense of calm throughout your nervous system, mind, and brain.

3. **Social connectivity.** Two studies published in the journal *Science* demonstrate that social aggression and isolation lead to increased levels

of cortisol that can trigger a cascade of potential mental health problems.

Relationships, whether it be family, friendship, or a romantic partner, are essential for your physical and mental health at any age. Recent studies have shown that the vagus nerve also responds to human connectivity and physical touch (oxytocin behaviors) to relax your parasympathetic nervous system.

The "tend-and-befriend" response is the exact opposite of the "fight-or-flight" response. The "tend-and-befriend" response increases oxytocin and reduces cortisol. Make an effort to spend real face-to-face time with loved ones whenever you can. Even phone conversations or Facebook engagement can reduce cortisol levels if they foster a feeling of genuine connectivity.

4. **Laughter, levity, and having fun** reduce cortisol levels. Many studies have shown the benefits of laughter, levity, and a sense of humor. Try to find as many opportunities as possible in your daily life to laugh and joke, and you'll lower your cortisol levels.

5. **Listening to music** that you enjoy and suits your mood has also been shown to lower cortisol levels. We all know the power of music to improve mood and reduce stress. Reducing your

cortisol levels is another reason to keep the music playing as a soundtrack for health and happiness in your life.

Chronic Stress Increases Serotonin

If you have a mood disorder, then you've probably heard the word "serotonin." Serotonin is a neurotransmitter responsible for regulating many of the functions in your body that contribute to your overall health and wellbeing.

This complex chemical exists everywhere in your body, but 95% of it is in your gut. When you are stressed all of the time, your nervous system undergoes chemical changes.

From Ray Peat, PhD in "Serotonin, depression, and aggression: The problem of brain energy":

> "Serotonin is regulated by the rate of its synthesis and degradation, by its uptake, storage and release, and by its transporters. In addition, its effects are modified by a great variety of receptors, by the number of these receptors, and by their binding affinities and competitive binders.
>
> "Different receptors 'are defined by the effects of chemicals other than serotonin; this means that serotonin itself hypothetically acquires some of the

properties of every substance that shows some binding competition with serotonin. This complexity has made it possible to argue that a given condition is caused by either an excess or a deficiency of serotonin."

Serotonin is known by other names including 5-HT (for its chemical name 5-hydroxytryptamine), thrombotonin, thrombocytin, and enteramine.

How Complicated Is Serotonin?

Here's what Ray Peat, PhD has to say about that in "Tryptophan, serotonin, and aging":

> *"Although several amino acids can be acutely or chronically toxic, even lethal, when too much is eaten, tryptophan is the only amino acid that is also carcinogenic. (It can also produce a variety of toxic metabolites and is very susceptible to damage by radiation). Since tryptophan is the precursor of serotonin, the amount of tryptophan in the diet can have important effects on the way the organism responds to stress, and the way an organism develops, adapts, and ages.*
>
> *"Serotonin excess produces a broad range of harmful effects: cancer, inflammation, fibrosis, neurological damage, shock, bronchoconstriction, and hypertension as examples. Increased serotonin impairs*

learning, serotonin antagonists improve it. "

Dr. Peat's list in that article is only a broad categorization of health problems caused by serotonin. The actual list of specific diseases and health issues involving serotonin is much longer.

The public's understanding of medicine is shaped by public relations through the introduction of words and concepts that frame the argument. Long before specific prescription drugs could be advertised directly to consumers, the medical and pharmaceutical industries were constructing a favorable framework for their products.

The success of corporate advertising can be observed in a recent article on serotonin which says, "It is a well-known contributor to feelings of well-being; therefore it is also known as a 'happiness hormone 'despite not being a hormone." **But there is no reliable research supporting this claim.**

That successful advertising was crafted for an audience with a sixth-grade level of education. Concepts such as bioelectronics and context-sensitive molecules like morphogenetic fields were just too complicated to explain easily or to sell well.

The difficulty with serotonin and chemicals like it is that they are state-dependent on sensitivities. The energetic state of a cell, and of the whole organism, determines the meaning of events and conditions, such as the presence of regulatory substances (which means that other substances regulate how serotonin reacts).

So, understanding how serotonin affects the body is dependent on understanding how serotonin itself is affected by a variety of individual factors. Some of these are other hormones and chemicals in the body, what medications are being taken and at what levels, and other external factors. **Increasing or decreasing the levels of serotonin in the body can and will have wildly varying effects depending on these other factors.**

The bottom line is uncertainty, and much more research is needed before anyone should be manipulating serotonin levels.

However, the pharmaceutical companies have been on a campaign to dumb down the explanation of how serotonin-enhancing drugs work. Instead of emphasizing the need to completely understand the environment that serotonin is operating in at any given time, the drug companies have boiled the message down to a discussion of selected molecular interactions. They don't say much at all about how the drugs increase the ability of serotonin to attach to specific chemical receptors in the human body.

While the limited view they present might be technically correct, it ignores the big picture and the big question: Should you even want to enhance your body's ability to transmit and/or produce more serotonin and its related chemicals? **Considering the research available to date (or the lack of research), the answer is almost certainly that you're better off with less rather than more serotonin in the body.**

Extremely huge misconceptions about the nature of the solar system didn't matter much until interplanetary travel became a possibility. And extremely serious misunderstandings about brain "transmitters" and "receptors" didn't matter much until the drug industry got involved.

"Three years before Prozac received approval by the US Food and Drug Administration in late 1987, the German BGA (that country's FDA equivalent) had such serious reservations about Prozac's safety that it refused to approve the antidepressant based on Lilly's studies showing that previously nonsuicidal patients who took the drug had a fivefold higher rate of suicides and suicide attempts than those on older antidepressants, and a threefold higher rate than those taking placebos." — *The Boston Globe*, 2000.

Ray Peat, PhD, points out in "Serotonin: Effects in disease, aging and inflammation:"

"Several kinds of research are now showing that the effects of the environment on the serotonergic system and its antagonists can influence every aspect of health, not just the personality.

"For example, there have been suggestions that early life isolation of an animal can affect its serotonergic activity and increase its anxiety, aggression, or susceptibility to stress (Malick and Barnett, 1976, Malick, 1979, dos Santos, et al, 2010) and these effects are associated with increased risk of becoming depressed, and developing organic problems."

He adds: *"In ... extreme conditions, serotonin reduces energy expenditure, eliminating all brain functions except those needed for simple survival."*

Since stress is known to increase levels of serotonin, and the many complex effects of serotonin on the body are not yet properly understood, **it makes much more sense to minimize stress, thereby minimizing serotonin.**

Histamine

Warning: " Histamine intolerance" is not a recognized medical diagnosis, so your doctor may not want to hear about it.

That doesn't mean there aren't known interactions between histamine, estrogen, the nervous system, stress, anxiety, and several other human body systems and processes.

What is Histamine?

Histamine is present in a wide range of tissues and organs in mammals. The concentration of histamine is different in different parts of the body, and it's an important bioactive chemical (a naturally occurring chemical that acts on a wide range of bodily functions).

One of the primary functions of histamine is conveying messages between the cells of the nervous system. It plays key roles in the regulation of stomach acids, the permeability of blood vessels, muscle contraction, and brain function. In humans, the highest histamine concentrations are found in the skin, lungs, and stomach, with smaller amounts in the brain and heart.

As long as it is balanced with other bodily activities, histamine is essential in defending the body against invasion by potentially disease-causing agents such as bacteria, viruses, and other foreign bodies.

When responding to potential threats to the body, histamine is always present when inflammation occurs.

Excess histamine causes inflammation.

Histamine plays many roles in the human body, including counteracting the symptoms of allergies, which in themselves are a form of inflammation. However, in the interest of remaining focused, I'm limiting my discussion on histamine here to its involvement with major bodily functions.

Histamine intolerance occurs when the body's normal processes for removing excess histamine from the body fail. When this happens, the level of histamine rises and creates symptoms that are, ironically, indistinguishable from the symptoms of allergies.

Symptoms that your body is not adequately clearing histamine from your system include:

❖ Hives

❖ Tissue swelling, particularly of the face and nasal/oral tissues including the throat

❖ Itchy skin, eyes, ears, and nose

❖ Red and watery eyes

❖ Nasal congestion and/or runny nose

❖ A drop in blood pressure

❖ A racing heart (increased pulse rate)

❖ Anxiety and panic attacks

❖ Chest pain

❖ Headaches (excluding migraine)

❖ Fatigue, confusion, and irritability

❖ Occasional short-term unconsciousness typically lasting only a few seconds

❖ Digestive tract irritability such as heartburn, indigestion, and acid reflux

The severity of these symptoms varies from one person to another, and they don't all have to be present to indicate histamine excess. However, the pattern of symptoms seems to be consistent for any given individual.

Important to know: Doctors hardly ever investigate excess histamine as a possible cause of nervous system problems although the nervous system is a major source of histamine.

Scientifically-Proven Roles of Histamine in the Nervous System

Because of the very large number of roles that histamine plays in the human body, it's not possible to cover all of them in this book. However, the roles directly related to the main theme of this book are outlined below:

Estrogen. Histamine plays a role in the release of the luteinizing hormones (hormones produced in the pituitary gland) that are involved in the production and regulation of estrogen and testosterone in men. Histamine and estrogen have an interdependent relationship: Histamine causes the release of estrogen, and estrogen causes the release of histamine.

Stress. Histamine is involved in the regulation of the body's functions and any physiological stress. Typical sources of physiological stress include dehydration, prolonged fasting, loss of blood, and severe infection. Any such stress results in the release of histamines as part of the body's defense system.

Additionally, when you are emotionally stressed histamine mediates the release of hormones and other neurotransmitters as part of the stress response.

Anxiety. A specific histamine receptor (H1R) is known to signal a danger response even when no perceivable danger is present (free-floating anxiety).

Metabolic Syndrome. Histamine regulates the hormone leptin, which in turn regulates the feeling of hunger. Improper function of this hormone can lead to obesity. Histamine levels also affect insulin resistance, diabetes, and cholesterol. Interestingly, chewing your food well induces activation of histamine neurons, which in turn suppresses food intake through H1R activation.

Stress is Your #1 Enemy

Most people think of stress as something that is caused by external environmental sources, things like an overbearing boss, a nagging spouse, financial problems, etc. But the fact is, we regularly experience internal physiological stressors — hormonal, enzyme, and chemical reactions inside of our bodies — that lead to physical stress.

There are many forms of stress that we never think about. Stress can be caused by the wrong kind of exercise for you, by eating unhealthy foods, by the short days and long nights of winter, and by many other things. Stress is your number one enemy and you need to learn to recognize it and manage it on multiple levels.

OXPHOS

All types of stress result in adverse physiological reactions in our bodies. One of the top two bad reactions is that it impedes oxidative phosphorylation (OXPHOS), the process by which cells use enzymes to oxidize nutrients to release the energy that is used to preform adenosine triphosphate (ATP).

Biologists consider ATP to be the energy currency of

life. It's the high-energy molecule that stores the energy we need to do just about everything. OXPHOS releases 30 to 35 ATP molecules for any given source of energy.

The OXPHOS process also enables the release of CO_2 into the body, which is good for organs, tissues, and oxygen absorption. Stress inhibits OXPHOS and therefore slows down efficient respiration.

An indication of poor OXPHOS processing is a buildup of lactic acid and high glycolysis. Conversion of glucose to lactic acid in the presence of oxygen is known as aerobic glycolysis or the "Warburg effect." Increased aerobic glycolysis is uniquely observed in cancers.

People suffering too much stress can experience glycolysis, which is an inefficient form of respiration in comparison to OXPHOS, releasing only five to eight molecules of ATP. It also limits the amount of CO_2 available to the body. Glycolysis can also be responsible for a "cancer metabolism" or "cancer respiration."

Obviously, you don't want that. If your stress causes glycolysis, your cells will suffer as will your overall health. Cancer metabolism goes downhill and causes metabolic "slow and low," low energy, low temperatures, low heart rate, and the inability to fight disease and cancer.

This is the reason stress is your #1 enemy.

By improving your body's OXPHOS processing, you will increase ATP production that brings about improved muscle power, mobility, flexibility, and endurance. The improved oxygen absorption elevates mitochondrial coupling, which raises both exercise efficiency and endurance in both young and old muscle. Both aspirin and drinking beetroot juice will improve your OXPHOS processing.

Internal Inflammation — Real Stress

Internal inflammation is the other major symptom of stress. The easiest explanation of internal inflammation to understand is "leaky gut". This is when your gut isn't performing correctly. Everyone's gut contains bacteria. But you need to ensure that your gut is hosting enough "good" bacteria and managing the amount of "bad" bacteria living there.

Leaky gut is a condition in which the bacteria get through your intestinal lining and attack other organs and tissues in your body. Many bodily functions that most of us take for granted may shut down in people with leaky gut because the body goes into survival mode to concentrate on fighting off the invasive bacteria attacking their organs.

When you don't have good health... for example, what's your body temperature? Do you feel cold? Do you have cold hands, feet, or nose? What is your heart rate? What is your pulse rate?

If you're feeling cold — especially if you have cold hands, cold feet, or a cold nose — that's a sign of low metabolism which is a metabolic problem I'm going to address. It's also a sign of cortisol metabolism, which I'm going to tell you how to fight and eliminate. Another sign of low metabolism is a low heart rate. Your resting heart rate should be around 70 to 85 beats per minute.

For many, it's 40 or 50 BPM, which indicates a very low metabolism, and that causes a lot of problems. How often do you urinate each day? Do you experience chronic thirst? Some people — especially men, but women too — are always peeing. Sometimes they get up several times through the night to pee. I know someone that pees 20 or 30 times a day.

All of these are signs of gut inflammation and internal inflammation. Of course, there are other possible reasons for these signs. For example, prostate inflammation could cause a man to pee more often because the prostate is pressing against the bladder, preventing it from completely emptying. However, quite often these symptoms are a result of gut inflammation, and I'm going to show you how to fix that.

How often do you have a bowel movement? Do you

suffer from constipation or bloating? Do you have gas often? Or diarrhea? What is your stool like? Is it runny, is it like pebbles, is it smelly? Does it have undigested food in it? The longer food stays in your gut before you have a bowel movement... Well, do you know what happens when food stays in your gut?

It rots, of course. Yeah, it ferments. It ferments and it rots. There's nothing we can do about that. That's the normal course of things. However, if the food passes through quickly there's a lot less rotting going on. With a higher metabolism, our food passes rapidly through our gut, and that reduces the amount of bacteria, yeast, and other things hanging around that we have to fight off.

And that's not just the bad bacteria, but both the good and the bad. Yeah, all of them, because they die, they fight each other, they cause what are called endotoxins (fragments of bacteria and chemicals from the bacteria) that get into our body and we have to continually fight off.

Endotoxins

Endotoxins are a huge contributor to inflammation, diabetes, heart disease, etc. The key to eliminating them is raising your metabolism so that, rather than sitting in your gut, food moves through your system quickly. On my program, you might go from having a bowel movement once a day to twice a day. You'll probably end up there and everything will become much easier and much more normal. By normal, I mean without artificial assistance such as laxatives.

How is your sleep? Restless, interrupted? Do you feel exhausted upon waking? Do you ever wake up at night with a pounding heart (you hear/feel your heart going boom, boom, boom)? Do you wake up frequently or do you sleep through the night and wake up refreshed? If you're not waking up refreshed, that means you're running on adrenaline and cortisol — what we call a cortisol metabolism — and you may also be low in thyroid hormones.

What about your hair, skin, and nails? Are they dry and brittle? Slow-growing? When you have a cut do you heal slowly? When your thyroid is under-active, a hormone called parathyroid slows healing and causes many problems in our body. Or you might be low in calcium, vitamin D3, and/or vitamin K2. You may be getting too much phosphorus with not enough magnesium or sodium to balance it. I'll show you how to fix all that.

How are your sex hormones? Could you care less if you ever have sex again? Do you have low libido? How's your energy? Are you dragging all day? Moody? Do you get sick often? Do you gain weight easily? These symptoms are almost always caused by the same things: gut inflammation and cortisol metabolism. **80% of your immune system function takes place in your gut because of all those**

bacteria that are in there (except when they leak out to your other organs).

You've probably learned something new about stress here. Stress is both mental and physiological. It's not always about trying to make the deadline for an important report at work, or other everyday activities. Much of your stress originates from within your body.

That is why so many of us have problems. And we're going to fix everything here. Everything!

We've Been Lied to About These Important Things

After our nervous system, our immune system is the most complicated system in our bodies. When our immune system is balanced and synchronized with the rest of our body, it performs two primary functions: fighting off external pathogens that are constantly trying to invade our bodies, and fighting our own cells that have mutated into an unhealthy form such as a cancer.

The amazing thing is that when your immune system is working well, you shouldn't even notice that it is active. But when the immune system it acting up, it wreaks havoc on various parts of your body. You may not understand what is going on in there but you can tell something isn't right. **The most common cause of the immune system running amok is leaky gut.**

When the Immune System Works Correctly

The immune system is constantly protecting the human body from attacks by bacteria, fungi, viruses, other pathogens, and foreign bodies.

The main tasks of the body's immune system are:

❖ Neutralizing and removing pathogens like bacteria, viruses, parasites, and fungi that enter the body.

❖ Recognizing and neutralizing harmful substances from the environment.

❖ Fighting against the body's own cells that have changed due to an illness —cancerous cells, for example.

Although the immune system does fight unhealthy cells produced by your own body, this is not the normal state. It's important for the immune system to recognize the difference between "self" and "non-self" cells, organisms, and substances.

An important misconception is that the immune system won't attack healthy cells. There are proteins on the surfaces of unhealthy cells that have special receptors that the immune system attaches to and begins the process of neutralizing or eliminating the unhealthy cells.

However, the body's healthy cells also have surface proteins. The immune system is not supposed to work against these cells. It's supposed to recognize these as "self." Autoimmune disease occurs when the immune system identifies the cells of its own body as "non-self."

When the Immune System Does NOT Work Correctly

Autoimmune disease affects up to 50 million Americans, according to the American Autoimmune Related Diseases Association (AARDA). Autoimmune disease typically causes inflammation of different parts of the body. Among the most common are:

❖ Inflammation of the intestines.

❖ Inflammation of the joints and surrounding tissues.

❖ Connective tissue disease that causes changes in skin, blood vessels, muscles, and internal organs.

❖ Inflammation of the thyroid gland.

❖ Inflammation of urethra and eyes which may cause sores on the skin and mucus membranes.

❖ Many other inflammatory symptoms.

The organs and tissues most commonly affected:

❖ Joints

❖ Muscles

❖ Skin

❖ Red blood cells

❖ Blood vessels

❖ Connective tissues

❖ Endocrine glands

Leaky Gut and Autoimmune Disease

According to the *Journal of Diabetes*, there is strong evidence pointing to leaky gut syndrome as a major cause of autoimmune diseases. **Leaky gut syndrome** has been gaining a lot of attention lately for several reasons:

❖ A growing body of research has linked leaky gut to a number of seemingly unrelated health concerns and chronic diseases.

❖ As more Americans are affected by poor diet choices, chronic stress, toxic overload, and bacterial unbalance, the prevalence of leaky gut seems to have reached epidemic proportions.

❖ **The medical profession is just now beginning to acknowledge that this condition even exists!**

What's particularly shocking is that "intestinal permeability" has been discussed in the medical literature for over 100 years! Yet, today's doctors aren't even aware of it. Meaning they can't tell you about it or treat it.

The father of modern medicine, **Hippocrates, said, "All disease begins in the gut,"** and modern research is only now proving that he was absolutely correct.

What the Medical Community Says About Leaky Gut

WebMD refers to leaky gut as "something of a medical mystery."

Could this be because it isn't even taught as a diagnosis in medical school!

According to gastroenterologist Donald Kirby, MD, Director of the Center for Human Nutrition at the Cleveland Clinic:

> *"From an MD's standpoint, it's a very gray area. Physicians don't know enough about the gut, which is our biggest immune system organ."*

Government agencies have also contributed to the confusion. According to the United Kingdom's National Health Service (NHS):

> *"There is little evidence to support this theory, and no evidence that so-called 'treatments' for 'leaky gut syndrome', such as nutritional supplements and a gluten-free diet, have any beneficial effect for most of the conditions they are claimed to help."*

A few forward-looking professionals are beginning to come around. In the words of Linda A. Lee, MD, gastroenterologist and Director of the Johns Hopkins Integrative Medicine and Digestive Center:

"We don't know a lot but we know that it exists. Nevertheless, in the absence of evidence, we don't know what it means or what therapies can directly address it."

Chronic Stress Helps You Kill You

Your body has a short-term solution for stress: the hormone cortisol and other corticosteroids. But chronic stress is a long-term condition. In the short term, the body's stress response is not a problem for your body. But long term exposure to the actions of cortisol and its associated chemicals will cause you serious physical damage. Cortisol supplements are another overly strong medicine with side effects that even medical doctors are hesitant to prescribe on a long-term basis.

There are two primary ways that stress has a direct, negative effect on the immune system:

1. It creates chronic inflammatory conditions.

2. It lowers the immunity of those who otherwise might have a healthy immune system.

According to Dr. Mary Meagher, PhD, Texas A&M University:

"People exposed to chronic social conflict experience high levels of stress and consequent dysregulation of the immune

system, thereby increasing vulnerability to infectious and autoimmune disease."

When cortisol is present in the blood for long periods, the body develops a resistance to cortisol and does not respond to it properly. Instead, **it actually ramps up production of substances that promote inflammation leading to a state of chronic inflammation.** These pro-inflammation substances, called cytokines, are associated with a host of chronic inflammatory and autoimmune conditions. When you have an autoimmune condition, your body basically mistakes itself as a threat and attacks itself.

Cortisol and corticosteroids suppress lymphocytes, a major component of the immune system. Lymphocytes kill invading organisms that would cause disease and recognize harmful substances to help defend against them.

With a decreased number of lymphocytes, the body is at increased risk of infection and disease and susceptible to contracting acute illnesses and suffering prolonged healing times.

When Your Body Turns on You

Clearly, you want your immune system to thrive so it can keep the rest of your body free of toxins, bad bacteria, and all of the pathogens that constantly attack. What you don't want is for your immune system to turn on you and begin damaging healthy organs and tissues.

Researchers are just now beginning to acknowledge that leaky gut even exists. The immune system is exactly that, a system. It is not a standalone organ that can easily be studied. Autoimmune diseases must be studied in a number of different environments to be fully understood. It will certainly be years before routine medical treatment will be available.

Even at that, we have seen how conventional medicine treats disease: It does it with strong medicines that bring on other complications. I don't think it will surprise anyone down the road when many of the medicines being prescribed today are shown to be the culprits behind many autoimmune diseases.

In the meantime, general healthy-living strategies are a good way to help give your immune system the upper hand. Following general guidelines for good health is the single best step you can take now to help keep your immune system strong and healthy. Every part of your body, including your immune system, functions better when protected from environmental assaults and bolstered by healthy-living strategies such as these:

❖ Don't smoke.

❖ Eat a wholesome and healthy diet free of the herbicides, pesticides, growth hormones, and other dangerous toxins common in today's commercial food chain.

❖ Stay active to get some exercise regularly.

❖ Maintain a healthy weight.

❖ If you drink alcohol, drink only in moderation.

❖ Get adequate sleep.

❖ Minimize or eliminate chronic stress (including internal stress).

❖ Take steps to avoid infection, such as washing your hands frequently and cooking meats thoroughly.

Cancer is NOT Genetic

Many people believe that cancers are genetically inherited from parents or other close blood relatives. For about 97% of cancer patients, this is simply not true. There is a genetic component to cancer, but that is almost never an inherited relationship. Just because your parents had/have cancer does not mean you are more likely to.

There is a reason that cancers develop more often in older people than in younger people. Most cancers are caused by gene flaws that develop during our lifetimes. These are typically caused by random errors during cell division.

Another cause that is much more common than heredity is exposure to environmental factors including smoking, sunlight, asbestos, radiation, and the many toxins we encounter daily in modern life.

Simply because a substance has been designated as a carcinogen, however, does not necessarily mean the substance will cause cancer. Many factors influence whether a person exposed to a carcinogen will develop cancer, including the extent, frequency, and duration of exposures and the health of the individual's immune system.

Gene mutations occur often, and the human body is normally able to correct most of them. Depending on where in the gene it occurs, a mutation may be beneficial, harmful, or have no effect at all. So, one gene mutation alone is unlikely to lead to cancer. Usually, it takes multiple mutations over a lifetime to cause cancer. This is why cancer occurs more often in older people — there has been more time for mutations to accumulate.

Cancer is Metabolic

Thomas Seyfried, PhD, is a professor of biology at Boston College and a leading expert and researcher in the field of cancer metabolism and nutritional ketosis. His book, *Cancer as a Metabolic Disease*, is an important contribution to the field of understanding how cancers start and can be treated. Seyfried's work is also heavily featured in Travis Christofferson's excellent book, *Tripping Over the Truth: The Metabolic Theory of Cancer.*

Every day, approximately 1,600 Americans die from cancer. Across the globe, the number is closer to 21,000. Many of these deaths are preventable and treatable.

Seyfried is a pioneer in using nutritional ketosis to treat cancer. His work is based on that of Dr. Otto Warburg, considered one of the most brilliant biochemists of the twentieth century and recipient of the Nobel Prize in Physiology or Medicine in 1931 for the discovery of metabolism of malignant cells.

Warburg also held a doctorate degree in chemistry and was friends with Albert Einstein and other outstanding scientists of the time. It's a complete mystery to me why Warburg's groundbreaking work wasn't followed up sooner and has been largely ignored by other researchers for decades.

Today, Seyfried is expanding on Warburg's early findings and has expanded Warburg's initial theory by shedding light on the metabolic underpinnings of cancer.

Seyfried's work has led him to conclude that Warburg's findings can be explored, not only as an approach for treating cancer, but also <u>for treating almost every disease known to man</u> — because mitochondrial dysfunction is at the core of most serious health conditions. As stated by Seyfried:

> "A dogma is considered irrefutable truth and that cancer is a genetic disease is, no question, a dogma. The problem with dogma is that sometimes it blinds you to alternative views and sets up ideologies that are extremely difficult to change.
>
> All of the major college textbooks talk about cancer as a genetic disease. On the National Cancer Institute (NCI) website, the first thing they say is cancer is a genetic disease caused by mutations... [and] if cancer is a genetic disease, everything flows from that concept.
>
> It permeates the pharmaceutical industry, academic industry, and textbook industry — the entire knowledge base. There's very little discussion of alternative views to the genetic view. The argument now is that, yes, metabolic problems occur in cancer cells. No one denies that.
>
> But these are all due to the genetic mutations. Therefore we must maintain ourselves on the established track that all of this metabolic stuff could be resolved if we just understood more about the genetic

underpinning of the disease.

Now that would be well and good if it were true. But evidence is accumulating that the mutations we see that are the prime focus and the basis for the genetic theory are actually epiphenomenal [a secondary or additional symptom or complication arising during the course of a disease].

There're downstream effects of this disturbance in the metabolism that Warburg originally defined back in the 1920s and '30s."

Winning the War on Cancer

The war on cancer moves slowly because the vast majority of the cancer industry is focused on the downstream effects of the problems (symptoms). But fighting symptoms does not solve the root problem. Seyfried says:

"Unfortunately, most of the cells in the tumor are all different from each other genetically. You're not going to be able to target all of the different cells using these kinds of approaches. Even though you may get success for a few months, or even a year in some people, the majority of people will not respond effectively to these kinds of therapies for the most part."

The treatments in use today are highly toxic. In fact, one of the big problems with today's treatments is that the patients are often too sick to take or survive the treatment. **When you view cancer as a metabolic disease, you can target and manage the disease without creating systemic toxicity.**

As explained by Seyfried, you do this by targeting the fuels the cancer cells are using:

> *"What we have to recognize...is that if cancer is a mitochondrial metabolic disease and you get cancer because of mitochondrial failure in certain populations of cells and certain tissues, if you prevent your mitochondria from entering into this dysfunctional state...[then] the probability of getting cancer is going to be significantly reduced.*
>
> *To what percent? I would say a minimum of 80 percent. Cancer is probably, as I said in my book, one of the most manageable diseases that we know of...*
>
> *The problem is that many people don't want [to take the preventive steps to avoid cancer]. They're like, 1 have to therapeutically fast for a week? Oh, I'm not going to. Give me a break. '... An effective prevention is to eat less and move more. A*

lot of people don't want to do that... Once you realize what cancer is, that it's a metabolic disease, you can take charge of those kinds of things. In other words, getting cancer is not God's will. It's not bad luck."

We need to consider the nutritional roots of cancer and other chronic disease, and you will hear a lot more about this in the months and years to come. Addressing mitochondrial dysfunction is the real key to solving most current health problems. <u>The good news is that optimizing mitochondrial function can be effectively accomplished through lifestyle strategies like a healthy diet and exercise. No costly drugs or invasive procedures required.</u>

Your Immune System Can Attack Cancer

Chemotherapy, biological therapies, and radiation therapy can temporarily weaken immunity by causing a drop in the number of white blood cells made in the bone marrow. High doses of steroids can also weaken your immune system while you are taking them.

The problem is that many people don't want to take the preventive steps to avoid cancer. Typically, they want an instant cure from strong medicines. They balk at the idea of therapeutically fasting for a week. An effective prevention is eating less and moving more. Does resisting that in favor of treatment with severe side effects sound familiar?

71

Fast for a week or suffer the terrible side effects of modern medicine —which do you think is harder on your body and more likely to kill you?

Once you realize what cancer is, that it's a metabolic disease, you can take charge of those kinds of things.

No costly drugs or invasive procedures required!

While there is still a long way to go, more doctors are starting to pay attention. "This is the tipping point," Seyfried says. "Many physicians are coming on board. I think things are going to start changing for the best and for the success of people."

Prostate Enlargement, Cancer, and Treatments

There are several other serious medical conditions that pharmaceutical companies have become addicted to profiteering from. Not to be outdone by Big Pharma, numerous law firms have also found ways to bring home the bacon through these multibillion-dollar opportunities. Rather than pushing these drugs on the public, these law firms specialize in civil class action suits to extract huge settlements from the pharmaceutical companies because of the severe side effects and physical damage (even death) caused by the drugs. Although some of that money goes to the suffering patients, the law firms collect very hefty fees for their services.

Have no doubt about it, there are staggering amounts of money to be made by generating fear in the public both coming and going. Often, a little knowledge will naturally overcome what ails people without pharma, doctors, or lawyers ever getting involved. But that's not what happens in our over-hyped culture, dominated as it is by mass media and big business.

Your Health and Internal Inflammation
Let's talk about what health looks like for a moment — good health. For example, let's go back to some

of the questions I asked earlier. What's your body temperature? Are your hands, feet, and nose cold? What is your heart rate? What is your pulse? If you're feeling cold, especially cold hands, cold feet and cold nose, that's a sign of low metabolism. That's a metabolic problem I'm going to address.

It's also a sign of cortisol metabolism, which I'm going to show you how to fight and eliminate. Having a low heart rate is actually also a sign of low metabolism. Your heart rate should be around seventy to eighty-five beats per minute at rest.

For many of us, our heart rate is forty or fifty, because we have a very low metabolism, which causes a lot of problems. How often do you urinate per day? Do you have chronic thirst? Some people, especially men, but women too are peeing all the time. Sometimes they get up at night several times to pee. I know someone who pees 20 or 30 times a day.

These are signs of gut inflammation, or the more serious concern, internal inflammation. There are other reasons for this problem. Prostate inflammation can cause a man to have to pee — the prostate is pressing in on his bladder and doesn't let him empty it when he does pee, so he has to pee all the time. But a lot of times it's gut inflammation, and I'm going to show you how to fix that.

Enlarged Prostate

Only men have a prostate gland. It is usually the shape and size of a walnut. An enlarged prostate is often called benign prostatic hyperplasia (BPH). **It is NOT CANCER** and it does not raise your risk for developing prostate cancer.

The prostate gland surrounds the urethra, the tube that carries urine from the bladder out of the body. As the prostate becomes enlarged, it may squeeze or partly block the urethra and this can cause problems with urinating.

Some studies have shown that obese men and men with diabetes may be more at risk of developing an enlarged prostate. You may be able to reduce your risk by being more active or getting some exercise. However, we still need more studies into the causes of this condition. A variety of factors may be involved, including androgens (male hormones), estrogens, growth factors, and other cell-signaling pathways.

Though many men with BPH (enlarged prostate) don't experience any symptoms, it can cause urinary problems such as:

❖ Trouble getting a urine stream started and completely stopped (dribbling).

❖ Often feeling like you need to urinate. This feeling may even wake you up at night.

❖ A weak urine stream.

❖ A sense that your bladder is not completely empty after you urinate.

In a small number of cases, BPH may cause the bladder to be blocked, making it impossible or extremely difficult to urinate. This problem may cause backed-up urine (urinary retention), leading to bladder infections or stones, or even kidney damage.

BPH does not cause prostate cancer and does not affect a man's ability to father children. **But it does cause erection problems.**

There are two classes of drugs currently approved to treat BPH: alpha-1 blockers and 5-alpha-reductase inhibitors. These work in entirely different ways and therefore present different types of problems. Simply put, alpha-1 blockers deal with the "going" problem by relaxing certain muscles in the prostate, and urinary tract and 5-alpha-reductase inhibitors deal with the "growing" problem by reducing the size of the prostate.

Before taking medications for an enlarged prostate, consider possible side effects. **There can often be sexual side effects to taking BPH medications.**

Prostate Treatments and ED

Because they affect levels of the male hormone testosterone, the 5-alpha-reductase inhibitors may cause a variety of sexual side effects. In clinical trials, 3.7% of men taking these drugs (4%-6% by some other estimates) developed erectile dysfunction (ED). Another 3.3% of men experienced a decline in libido, while 2.8% had problems ejaculating during orgasm.

In addition, one of the selective alpha-1 blockers (tamsulosin) causes ejaculation problems in some men who take it. (The other alpha-1 blockers are not as likely to have this side effect.)

While those individual numbers look relatively low, they still constitute a large number of men experiencing ED thanks to the strong drugs. And that's not taking into account any other drugs that you also might be taking. Beginning with the drugs that are prescribed to overcome ED caused by the prostate drugs — Viagra, Cialis, and Levitra — the combinations and potential for side effects are mind-numbing.

Prostate Massage for BPH

A Columbia University Medical Center study had promising results for improving urination in men with BPH using a medical grade prostate massage devise (Pro-State®, High Island Health). The study focused on lower urinary tract symptoms (LUTS) related to bladder emptying, dribbling, etc.

This study was for at-home use after finding positive results from an in-office prostatic massage. The results for 115 men with an average age of 64.48 composed the study results. Device use ranged from less than four weeks to greater than twenty-four weeks. Pain, urinary function, and quality of life were the primary metrics, along with frequency and duration of use. Significant results demonstrate that the application of an at-home-use prostate massage device may relieve LUTS in men with BPH (and CP/CPPS). However, dosage with regard to frequency and duration needs to be determined, and monitoring of safety must be considered.

Rib Roast Procedure

UroLift (prostatic urethral lift) is a minimally invasive process where they tie up your prostate like a butcher ties a rib roast. Rather than surgery, the procedure is performed directly through the penis. Unlike drugs and BPH surgeries, it spares sexual functioning (UroLift prevents retrograde ejaculation).

Doctors use tiny implants and sutures to pull the prostate away from the bladder so that urine flows more freely out of the body. The procedure is usually performed in a doctor's office. Most men go home the same day without a catheter. The results can be expected to last at least five years. This is one of the newest procedures. The FDA approved UroLift in 2013 and the American Urological Association began recommending it in 2018. Urologists are now up to speed on the procedure. If you decide this is an option for you, you should look for a surgeon that has performed it at least a dozen times.

NEW: Focused Ultrasound Treatment

Focused ultrasound is the newest treatment intended to treat BPH fibrosis. It's an early-stage, noninvasive, therapeutic technology with the potential to improve the quality of life and decrease the cost of care for patients with BPH. Focused ultrasound is a noninvasive alternative to surgery with less risk of complications such as surgical wound healing or infection.

This technology focuses beams of ultrasound energy precisely and accurately on targets in the prostate without damaging surrounding normal tissue. Where the beams converge, focused ultrasound produces precise ablation (thermal destruction of tissue) enabling BPH to be treated without surgery.

Access to this new technology is limited but treatment for BPH is approved in the US, Canada, China, Europe, India, Japan, Korea, Middle East, Russia, and South America. Studies are on going and no data is yet available about sexual function.

Surgery and Radiation as BPH Alternatives

It seems that almost every year, a new surgical option is introduced to treat BPH. A big part of the reason that new procedures keep coming out is because the existing ones produce poor results and have terrible side effects. Yet, doctors keep pushing these instead of telling men to correct the root problem with a natural solution that requires healthier living.

There are healthy alternatives for BPH surgery and invasive procedures but if you and your doctor are considering these, you're going to want to first do in-depth research on these common procedures:

Transurethral resection of the prostate (TURP) is the most common surgery and is often referred to as the "Roto-Rooter" technique. The surgeon threads an instrument called a resectoscope through the penis to the prostate, then uses the electrical loop to cut away the overgrown tissue that's pressing against the urethra.

Green Light procedure (also known as PVP) is newer than TURP and considered more advanced. The surgeon threads a thin tube known as a cystoscope into the urethra and up into the enlarged prostate. The surgeon then threads a fiber-optic device through the cystoscope to generate high-intensity pulses of laser light, which simultaneously vaporize the obstructing tissue and cauterize it to reduce bleeding.

Transurethral microwave thermotherapy (TUMT) uses heat to destroy prostate tissue by guiding a thin catheter carrying a miniature microwave generator through the penis to the prostate. This procedure can be performed on an outpatient basis.

Transurethral needle ablation (TUNA) is a newer thermal approach using low-level radio waves delivered through twin needles to heat and kill obstructing prostate cells. This one can also be performed on an outpatient basis.

Here are a few representative comments from men that have undergone these invasive surgeries:

❖ "I continue to have recurring prostate bleeding with clots, blockage for 1-2 weeks per episode, with clear urine for 3-5 weeks in between. My original surgeon indicated he hasn't seen this before, and has recommended a 2nd PVP, and, in contrast, a referral surgeon indicated bleeding can only stopped with a TURP."

❖ "Had turp 4 yrs ago at age 62 as i could not urinate. bph and large prostrate. In last 18 months needed a cath..something I hate..about 6 times. Scheduled green light for early April. Will trade the sexual side effects to hopefully never need another foley."

❖ "Don't do it! I had the green light procedure
   about 5 years ago. No pain and can pee a stream
   8 foot without straining BUT I now suffer from
   retrograde ejaculation and no complete sexual
   satisfaction or orgasam. Erection is good but
   just no release. The doctor didn't address this
   before and now downplaying the results.
   Just say NO!"

Almost all men undergoing surgery or radiation
treatment for an enlarged prostate suffer nerve
irritation that causes ED. Of those who emerge from
surgery or radiation with intact nerves, most will
see substantial improvement within a year.

By that point, about 40-50% of men who have
undergone a nerve-sparing version of a
prostatectomy will have returned to their pre-
treatment function. After two years, about 30%-60%
will have returned to pre-treatment function.

For those who undergo radiation therapy, the
numbers are better initially but tend not to improve
much over time. About 25%-50% of men who
undergo brachytherapy experience ER as do nearly
50% of men who have standard external beam
radiation treatment.

After two to three years, few men will see much of
an improvement and occasionally these numbers

worsen over time, given that radiation takes longer to cause side effects.

Men who undergo procedures that are not designed to minimize side effects and/or those whose treatments are administered by physicians who are not proficient in the procedures will fare worse. In addition, men with other diseases or disorders that impair their ability to maintain an erection, such as diabetes or vascular problems, will have a more difficult time returning to pre-treatment function.

<u>Do you want to go two or more years without sex or, worse, do you want to be one of the men who never regains sexual health/function or who goes for years without being able to have an erection?</u>

Not me!

BPH Progresses Slowly

Because BPH (as a symptom) progresses slowly and serious complications are uncommon, **most men can decide for themselves if and when they should be treated.** And many men with mild to moderate symptoms find that **simple lifestyle adjustments can take the BPH nuisance out of their daily life entirely.** Here are a few tips:

❖ Read on to learn how to rid yourself of intestinal inflammation to help resolve these problems.

And/Or:

❖ Reduce your intake of fluids, particularly after the evening meal.

❖ Limit your intake of alcohol and caffeine, and avoid them after mid-afternoon. Both are diuretics that increase urine production.

❖ Avoid medications that stimulate muscles in the bladder neck and prostate. Pseudoephedrine and other decongestants are the chief culprits.

❖ If you are taking diuretics for high blood pressure or heart problems (or some other health issue), work with your doctor to try to reduce the dose by reducing and eliminating intestinal inflammation.

Enlarged prostate and prostate cancer are NOT the same thing...

Prostate Cancer

First of all, just because you have symptoms doesn't mean you have prostate cancer. Even if you do have prostate cancer, it doesn't necessarily need to be treated. Many prostate cancers grow very slowly or not at all, and even go away on their own.

100% of men with BPH have internal inflammation. Doctors no longer talk about this because people don't want to make lifestyle changes.

Here are a few myths you need to disregard:

Myth #1: If you have prostate symptoms, it's likely to be cancer.

NOT True. There are many conditions of the prostate gland that are not cancer, including the following:

❖ **Prostatism**: any condition of the prostate that causes interference with the flow of urine from the bladder.

❖ **Prostatitis**: inflammation that may be accompanied by discomfort, pain, frequent or infrequent urination, and sometimes fever.

❖ **Prostatalgia**: pain in the prostate gland.

❖ **BPH**: enlargement of the prostate (benign prostatic hyperplasia). BPH is the most common non-cancerous prostate problem. It can cause discomfort and problems with urinating. BPH symptoms can be alarming because they are often similar to those of prostate cancer. **Note:** BPH is frequently overcome by eliminating intestinal inflammation.

❖ **ED**: inability to achieve or maintain an erection.

❖ **Urinary incontinence**: loss of bladder control.

Myth #2: Prostate cancer almost always happens in older men.
NOT True. Many men diagnosed with prostate cancer in their late 40s and 50s react with disbelief. They think that prostate cancer only happens after the age of 65. Older men do in fact have a higher risk of prostate cancer (again, it often goes away on its own, grows very slowly, stops growing, or simply causes few or no problems). However, younger men can also develop the disease. This is just one more reason to take care of your health.

Myth #3: Expect to develop ED if you have an enlarged prostate.
Not true, again. There is little or no correlation between an enlarged prostate and cancer, and ED is much less likely without invasive cancer treatment (including radiation treatment), though it can be a result of the same problems that cause BPH or prostate cancer (think inflamed gut here).

Myth #4: "It runs in the family." If your father, uncles, grandfathers, and other male blood relatives developed prostate cancer, you probably will also.

More falsehood. Lifestyle (especially diet) is the key cause of prostate cancer and an inflamed gut is where you want to begin. Studies show that junk food, industrialized meat products, foods infused with processed sugar, and other modern diet abnormalities heighten the risk factor significantly.

It makes sense that eliminating or significantly reducing these bad foods from your diet is your best choice, regardless of family history. In reality, the family history link may be a common poor diet.

There are many myths and falsehoods about prostate cancer out there. Always question these and do your own research. **Look for the most recent information, because this field is evolving fast and few doctors stay current with it.**

Prostate Cancer is Slow-Growing

In many cases, prostate cancer stops growing, is slow-growing, does not reduce life expectancy, and may not need treatment. Prostate cancer is different from most other cancers because small areas of cancer within the prostate are actually very common. These may not grow or cause any problems for many years (if at all).

Prostate cancer is often very slow-growing and for many men with prostate cancer, the disease never progresses or even causes any symptoms.

In other words, many men with prostate cancer will never need any treatment.

You should be fully aware that, like many medical treatments, treatment for prostate cancer can cause several side-effects, and one of those is ED.

Note: many autopsy studies show that many older

men (and some younger men) who died of other causes also had prostate cancer that never caused them problems. In many cases, neither the man nor his doctors even knew he had it.

According to a *New York Times* report:

> *"Fortunately, prostate cancer tends to be slow growing compared to other cancers. As many as 90% of all prostate cancers remain dormant and clinically unimportant for decades. Most older men eventually develop at least microscopic evidence of prostate cancer, but it often grows so slowly that,* ***many men with prostate cancer 'die with it, rather than from it.'"***

Dr. Otis Brawley, Chief Medical Officer of the American Cancer Society:

> *"We're finding that about 25 to 30 percent of some cancers stop growing at some point, that can make some treatments look good that aren't doing anything. Until doctors figure out how to identify which patients have cancers that won't progress, the only option is to treat everyone."*

Really? How about NOT treating them until it's shown to be needed?

Other research indicates that men who are diagnosed with low-grade prostate cancers have a minimal risk of dying from prostate cancer for up to 20 years after diagnosis. That's plenty of time to monitor progress.

Prostate Cancer Goes Away

Our immune systems are responsible for the formation and the disappearance of many tumors. Our health care system is so primitive it's sickening (literally and figuratively). It's just shocking that, while billions are spent on finding a pharma cure for cancer, nothing is spent on encouraging or even studying natural remission.

Actually, no, it's not shocking. There's no money in natural remission.

The focus of cancer research should be in finding ways to enhance the body's own ability to cure/reverse cancer. The ideal would be following people in whom this process is happening and to study it at a molecular level.

But that kind of study isn't happening. Why? Because the prevailing attitude says it's "impossible."

Let's face it, there are big bucks in radiation and chemo. And most of the practitioners are wealthy men who are in their comfort zone and don't want to be disturbed.

The holistic health movement has been saying this kind of thing for the better part of a century now and it's mostly fallen on deaf ears... Finally, though, a wee bit of truth is emerging.

But the fact remains, so long as our health care system is based on selling expensive treatments that don't work, there are few incentives to truly cure diseases on the cheap.

There is no greater threat to the medical/cancer complex than the possibility that a properly nourished body, often with supplements of special vitamins and minerals to specifically counter cancer, might make many high-tech cancer interventions — e.g., surgery, radiation, and chemo — unnecessary and possibly seen as more harmful than beneficial.

Prostate Cancer Treatments Have Severe Side Effects

Even the tests used for early detection actually stimulate cancers through radiation, cutting, and poisons. On top of that, doctors frequently discover anomalies during testing that would naturally disappear if left alone. They always treat those anomalies and the patients almost always die from the treatments.

So, these days, people are dying from the treatments instead of from the cancers, and this is demonstrated in the medical establishment's own statistics. Whenever a body is exposed to chemotherapy, cancers will strike sooner or later regardless of whether they existed initially. All chemotherapy drugs are carcinogenic, and they weaken all healthy cells. This is admitted in the official literature describing adverse effects for all of the so-called anti-cancer medical treatments.

Still, massive cellular destruction is officially a part of standard treatments by design. The claim is that the medicines attack the weaker cancer cells, but they do that by attacking all of the cells and thereby the very immune system that is so critical for recovery.

The success rate for curing cancer is not going to go up much through conformist medicine because of the unwillingness to consider less profitable methodologies. A rise in the success statistics for orthodox cancer treatments would indicate a change in the methods of calculating cure rates, not a change in actual survival rates. That's how the books of modern medicine are cooked.

Surviving for a mere five years is currently counted as a successful cure, but patients usually die before the 10-year mark. In accounting circles, this is called "cooking the books."

Most people are shocked when they learn that those

who die during drug trials are excised from the records, because the departed "did not complete the study." Dying during an experimental drug trial actually helps a drug company's chance of getting that drug approved, because those who get the sickest are not counted.

> "Success of most chemotherapies is appalling... There is no scientific evidence for its ability to extend in any appreciable way the lives of patients suffering from the most common organic cancer... Chemotherapy for malignancies too advanced for surgery, which accounts for 80% of all cancers, is a scientific wasteland."
>
> — Dr. Ulrich Abel

The known side effects of prostate cancer treatment are far-reaching. More alarmingly, **unknown side effects** are certain to be adding to the already overwhelming list of known complications. Though far from being an all-inclusive list, here are some of the categories of complications: medicine interactions, physical, social, emotional, and sexual side effects. In addition, side effects can be either short-term or long-term. While you're not likely to suffer all of the possible side effects, you'll almost certainly experience a bunch of them.

Active surveillance involves lots of ongoing testing,

some of which is not reliable. While some procedures are noninvasive, others, such as biopsies of the prostate, are invasive. Common side effects of active surveillance include ED and urinary incontinence. Biopsies pose the risk of causing infection.

Watchful waiting may be an option for much older men and those with other serious or life-threatening illnesses who are expected to live less than five years. With watchful waiting, routine PSA tests, DRE, and biopsies are not usually performed. If a patient develops symptoms from the prostate cancer, such as pain or blockage of the urinary tract, then more advanced treatment may be recommended, but runs the risk of causing complications due to the other illnesses.

Surgery is the removal of the tumor and some surrounding healthy tissue during an operation. There are multiple types of surgery that might be performed, and each carries its own risks.

❖ **Radical (open) prostatectomy** is the surgical removal of the entire prostate and the seminal vesicles. Lymph nodes in the pelvic area may also be removed. If you undergo this operation, you run the serious risk of impeding your sexual function.

Nerve-sparing surgery (when this is an option) increases the chance that a man can maintain his sexual function after surgery by avoiding surgical damage to the nerves that facilitate erection and orgasm. To help resume normal sexual function, men can receive drugs, penile implants, or injections.

Urinary incontinence is another possible side effect, which is sometimes treated with another surgery... more bad medicine on top of the first bad medicine.

❖ **Robotic or laparoscopic prostatectomy** is similar to radical prostatectomy (above) in that the entire prostate and healthy surrounding tissues are removed. The ED and urinary incontinence side effects are also similar. However, the patient may experience a shorter recovery time, less bleeding, and less pain.

❖ **Cryosurgery** (also called cryotherapy or cryoablation) is the freezing of cancer cells with a metal probe inserted through a small incision in the area between the rectum and the scrotum. There are many unknowns regarding this surgery and it is not at all clear what effect it may have on urinary and sexual function.

❖ **Radiation therapy** involves the use of high-energy rays to destroy cancer cells. The types of radiation therapy used to treat prostate cancer include:

◆ **External-beam radiation therapy** is the most

94

common type of radiation treatment. Some cancer centers use conformal radiation therapy (CRT) in which the radiation is beamed from different directions to focus the dose on the tumor.

♦ **Intensity-modulated radiation therapy (IMRT)** is a type of external-beam radiation therapy that uses CT scans to form a three-dimensional (3D) picture of the prostate before treatment. With IMRT, high doses of radiation are supposed to be directed at the prostate without increasing the risk of damaging nearby organs.

♦ **Proton therapy** (also called proton beam therapy) is a type of external-beam radiation therapy that uses protons rather than x-rays. At high energy levels, protons can destroy cancer cells. Current research has not shown that proton therapy provides any more benefit to men with prostate cancer than traditional radiation therapy. It is also more expensive.

♦ **Brachytherapy** (or internal radiation therapy) is the insertion of radioactive sources directly into the prostate. These sources, called seeds, give off radiation just around the area where they are inserted and may be used for hours (high-dose rate) or for weeks (low-dose rate). Low-dose rate seeds are left in the prostate permanently, even after all the radioactive material is supposed to have been used up. For a patient with a high-risk cancer, brachytherapy is usually combined with other treatments.

♦ **Radium-223** is a radioactive substance that is naturally attracted to areas of high bone turnover (areas where bone is being destroyed and replaced at a higher rate than what is normal). Radium-223 delivers radiation directly to tumors found in bone, limiting damage to healthy tissue. According to the results of a clinical trial published in 2013, treatment with radium-223 reduced bone-related complications and improved survival rates.

Radiation therapy may cause immediate side effects such as diarrhea or other problems with bowel function, such as gas, bleeding, and loss of control of bowel movements, as well as increased urinary urgency and frequency, fatigue, ED, rectal discomfort, burning, or pain. Most of these side effects usually fade away after treatment, **but ED is usually permanent**.

<u>Many other side effects of radiation therapy may not show up until months or years after treatment.</u>

❖ **Androgen deprivation therapy (ADT)** involves lowering the level of male sex hormones called androgens, which are believed to drive the growth of prostate cancer. The most common androgen is testosterone.

Testosterone levels in the body can be lowered by either surgically removing the testicles (surgical castration), or administering drugs that turn off the function of the testicles (medical castration). Doesn't that sound like a treatment to look forward to?

The chemical form of ADT for treating prostate cancer is often used in combination with surgery and/or radiation. Just think of it as a prostate cancer treatment cocktail. Specific variations include:

❖ **Bilateral orchiectomy** is the surgical removal of both testicles. Although this is a surgery, it is considered an ADT because it removes the main source of testosterone production in the body. The effects of this surgery are permanent and cannot be reversed.

❖ **LHRH agonists** are hormonal treatments in which luteinizing hormone-releasing hormone (LHRH) agonists are used to prevent the testicles from receiving messages sent by the body to make testosterone. By blocking these signals, LHRH agonists reduce a man's testosterone level just as well as removing his testicles.

However, unlike surgical castration, the effects of LHRH agonists are reversible, so testosterone production usually begins again once a patient stops treatment. LHRH may temporarily increase the activity of prostate cancer cells and cause symptoms and side effects, such as bone pain in men with cancer that has spread to the bone.

❖ **LHRH antagonists** are a different class of drugs from LHRH agonists though both involve the manipulation of how receptors behave. Also known as gonadotropin-releasing hormone (GnRH) antagonists, these chemicals also prevent the testicles from producing testosterone but they reduce testosterone levels more quickly and do not cause the temporary increase of prostate cancer cell activity. One possible side effect of this treatment is severe allergic reaction.

❖ **Anti-androgens** differ from LHRH agonists and antagonists in that they block testosterone from binding to so-called androgen receptors — chemical structures in cancer cells that allow testosterone and other male hormones to enter the cells.

There are also combinations of these drugs that are used in the treatment of prostate cancer. Often the combination treatments include other drugs that inhibit testosterone production in other parts of the body, such as the adrenal glands.

These drugs are often taken two, four, or more times a day.

As you certainly realize, eliminating testosterone production is going to lead to ED and a very low libido.

Besides those, other common side effects are high blood pressure, low blood potassium levels, fluid retention, weakness, joint swelling or pain, swelling in the legs and/or feet, hot flushes, diarrhea, vomiting, shortness of breath, and anemia. **No one knows the complete list of possible side effects.** However, obesity, heart disease, stroke, and diabetes are also known side effects.

This is on top of any side effects caused by strong medications you may be taking for other conditions.

Chemotherapy is the use of drugs to destroy cancer cells, usually by inhibiting their ability to grow and divide. There are several different drugs that are used for chemotherapy.

Side effects of chemotherapy depend on the individual, the type of chemotherapy received, the dosage used, and the duration of treatment. They can include fatigue, sores in the mouth and throat, diarrhea, nausea and vomiting, constipation, blood disorders, nervous system complications, changes in thinking and memory, sexual and reproductive issues, loss of appetite, pain, and hair loss.

Prostate Cancer and ED

There is a growing body of evidence demonstrating that, while early treatment with surgery or radiation prevents relatively few men from dying of prostate cancer, it leaves many with urinary or erectile problems and other side effects. As a result, more men may be willing to consider the active surveillance strategy, in which doctors monitor low-risk cancers closely and consider treatment only when the disease threatens to grow and spread.

Assuming intimacy and sex are important to patients before prostate cancer treatment, these can remain priorities and sex can remain enjoyable after prostate cancer treatment. It's up to each individual man and his partner how they want to move forward with sex and intimacy.

After prostate cancer treatment, intimacy and sex can still be enjoyable, though they may be different. Most men who have undergone prostate surgery or radiation without androgen deprivation therapy will continue to have a normal sex drive.

So, the desire for sex is still there but the mechanics of getting an adequately blood-filled engorged penis may no longer cooperate for some men.

Some men also notice penile shrinkage after

surgery, which is thought to be related to decreased muscle tone immediately following surgery followed by muscle atrophy due to lack of erections. The shrinkage can be transient, but, if erections do not return, it can be permanent.

On the slightly more positive side, the nerves responsible for the climax sensation are closer to the surface than the nerves responsible for erections, and so most men will continue to enjoy the climax feeling, even without an erection.

Although most men are able to and continue to enjoy orgasm/climax after prostate cancer treatment, some men describe the climax sensation as diminished though still enjoyable (though some describe it as similar to before treatment).

After that depressing discussion, let's take a look at some more encouraging news...

Estimation of Prostate Cancer Risk is Inaccurate

Relax a bit! The better news is that the risk of prostate cancer is exaggerated and the diagnosis is often inaccurate.

In its first twenty years of use, the prostate-specific antigen (PSA) screening test for prostate cancer has successfully reduced prostate cancer mortality. But it has also led to significant **over-diagnosis and**

over-treatment. The fact that this happens is widely known, but the exact statistics are not. Nor is this information widely shared with the very men being diagnosed or undergoing treatment.

As a result, many men are subjected to unnecessary prostate biopsies and over-treatment of slow or non-growing (indolent) cancers in order to save a small number of men from dying of prostate cancer.

Most men diagnosed with prostate cancer have a tumor that is unlikely to pose a threat to his life. A recent systematic analysis suggested that **up to 60% of prostate cancers diagnosed in current studies can be safely observed without a need for an immediate biopsy.**

In the United States, because of the concern for possible underestimation of prostate cancer severity due to biopsy sampling error, **90% of men diagnosed with prostate cancer undergo treatment and approximately 66% will be confirmed to have slow or non-growing prostate cancer.** This confirms a significant problem with overtreatment.

Although treatment for localized prostate cancer provides excellent cancer control, this comes with a significant sacrifice to quality of life for many. Studies have reported significant diminishment in life quality after primary treatment for prostate cancer. Life quality deterioration occurs primarily in the areas of sexual or urinary function or both.

Yet, medical professionals consider these physical and psychological impairments to be secondary adverse events. <u>Out of lack of concern for these side effects, doctors and specialist err on the side of positive diagnoses followed by treatment.</u> **Fortunately, many patients are beginning to question the benefits and weigh the risks of prostate cancer screening and treatment.**

It's clear that new biomarkers or tests that improve the detection of low-growth or no-growth cancer are unlikely to be forthcoming. Instead, big pharma and prostate specialists have decided that we need tests focusing on the detection of aggressive tumors, not the low-risk ones that are better left alone.

Those are NOT the only major health issues the entrenched medical profession has misled us about.

Read on...

Other Serious Medical Issues We Are Misguided About

What do you think is the most dangerous and harmful practice of pharmaceutical companies? If you follow the experts who are trying to shine a light on the truth about modern drugs that do more harm than good, you know it's the fact that **those with the most to gain financially from the drug industry make active and on-going efforts to suppress and outright hide the results of clinical studies that show their products in a negative light.**

Studies with negative findings are not published nor are they even shared with anyone without a "need to know." This includes professionals within their own companies and certainly "outsiders" such as doctors and even government agencies with oversight responsibilities.

This practice is so pervasive that even published studies with positive results routinely disregard participants who died during the study on the basis that these people did not complete the study.

Ben Goldacre's book, *Bad Pharma: How Drug Companies Mislead Doctors and Harm Patients*, cites as one example the antidepressant reboxetine, of which only one trial out of seven in which it was tested against a placebo was published. The published trial showed it to be effective; the other six, involving many more patients, remain unpublished.

Other unpublished trials, in which it was compared to selective serotonin reuptake inhibitors, **suggested that, contrary to the conclusions of the few published trials, it was less effective and had worse side effects than other drugs intended for the same purpose.**

Misunderstandings About Blood Pressure

High blood pressure, also known as hypertension, affects nearly one/third of all Americans, according to current medical standards. Hypertension is a condition in which too much force (blood pressure) is exerted on arteries and organs.

A blood pressure reading consists of two measurements. Systolic pressure is the maximum pressure, when the heart contracts to pump blood through the body. The second measurement is diastolic pressure, the minimum pressure, when the heart is at rest.

Current medical standards define "normal" blood pressure as a systolic pressure reading between 90 and 120 (millimeters of mercury — mm Hg), with a diastolic pressure reading between 60 and 80.

Although this is a medical standard, the guidelines have NOT been static. The guidelines referenced above (120/80) came out in **2013**. This is not accepted by all experts in the field. In a nutshell, here is what many experts recommend:

❖ Among adults age 60 and older with high blood pressure, aim for a target blood pressure under 150/90.

❖ Among adults age 30 to 59 with high blood pressure, aim for a target blood pressure under 140/90.

❖ Among adults with diabetes or chronic kidney disease, aim for a target blood pressure under 140/90.

Under the latest guidelines (2015) the goal is a lower systolic (top number) pressure to about 140-150 for people over 60 years old. The 2015 blood pressure guidelines support this more relaxed threshold and call for treatment to lower blood pressure to 150/90 mm Hg for people over age 60, and to 140/90 for adults younger than 60.

Uhhh... stay tuned: A newer study called SPRINT (Systolic Blood Pressure Intervention Trial) , which was supposed to end in **2017**, has been concluded early with findings suggesting a systolic pressure **below 120** reduces the risk of heart attack and stroke by up to 1/3, and risk of death by up to 1/4.

However, many studies over the years have found it's very hard to prove any benefit as a result of lowering systolic blood pressure below 130 for someone over 60 years of age. In fact, while a systolic pressure that is naturally 120 may be good for some, it is quite another matter to artificially drag someone's blood pressure down this low with blood pressure medications. It's as simple as the fact that not all people are physiologically the same.

Bad Medicine — Big Money

Setting a lower target means prescribing more and more medications to more and more people (benefitting Big Pharma). Other studies show that hundreds and hundreds... no, thousands and tens of thousands and probably **millions of people, would need to be put on these medicines to prevent heart attacks and strokes for a few.** This is known as **"number needed to treat"** (NNT).

The accepted NNT for use of a statin drug is 104. This means that for every 104 people who take a statin, **only one person has a heart attack prevented! Please read that AGAIN.** 104 people are put at risk for adverse side effects caused by statin drugs to prevent a heart attack in one person!

Facts show that as many as 1 out of 10 people are harmed by statin drugs. While considering the large numbers of people being exposed to this harm, keep in mind that a substantial number of them are the frail elderly who are at risk for falls and have other health issues, and others who are already taking an array of drugs for other chronic conditions and therefore are at risk of the further danger of drug interactions.

Now, look at the fact that the lowered standards for blood pressure mean that Big Pharma will sell much, much more of their expensive and dangerous medications. **I seriously don't think public health is best served by this.**

Elderly May Be at Risk Due to Low Blood Pressure

Blood pressure targets set too low are not a big help to the elderly. Neurologists worry that when blood pressure is too low the flow of blood to the brain is reduced, which may contribute to fainting, dizziness, and falls among older people.

Dr. Clifford Saper, professor of neurology at Harvard Medical School and Beth Israel Deaconess Medical Center, says that neurologists are already noting that blood pressure for some patients has been adjusted to the point where it becomes too low to support blood flow to the brain.

Good for elderly dementia, right? **Certainly — there is another expensive drug to fix that!**

Blood pressure fluctuates all the time, hour by hour and day by day, resulting in over-diagnosis and unnecessary treatment of millions of people. In fact, it's not uncommon for blood pressure to rise simply in response to a doctor's visit! This is called the "white coat syndrome" and it has been documented repeatedly.

High Blood Pressure Medicines

There are a slew of high blood medications on the market. The Center for Disease Control estimates that 70 million adult Americans have high blood pressure. That is a huge pie for BIG PHARMA to go after with their overly expensive and dangerous medicines. And go after it is what they've done. Without considering those drugs that are just emerging onto the market or are still in clinical trials, the list includes:

❖ **Diuretics:** reduce sodium and fluid in the body by increasing urination (every older man wants to pee more). This lowers blood pressure by lowering blood volume. Mild hypertension can sometimes be treated using diuretics alone, although they are more commonly used in combination with other medications intended for high blood pressure (think interactions here). Examples of diuretics include:

◆ Bumetanide (Bumex)

♦ Chlorthalidone (Hygroton) Chlorothiazide (Diuril)

♦ Ethacrynate (Edecrin)

♦ Furosemide (Lasix)

♦ Hydrochlorothiazide HCTZ (Esidrix, Hydrodiuril, Microzide)

♦ Indapamide (Lozol)

♦ Methyclothiazide (Enduron)

♦ Metolazone (Mykroz, Zaroxolyn)

♦ Torsemide (Demadex)

❖ **Beta blockers:** lower blood pressure by acting directly on the heart. These high blood pressure medications reduce heart rate and the force of the heart's pumping. They also reduce blood volume. Beta blockers include:

♦ Acebutolol (Sectral)

♦ Atenolol (Tenormin)

♦ Bisoprolol fumarate (Zebeta)

♦ Carvedilol (Coreg): combined alpha/beta blocker

- Esmilol (Brevibloc)

- Labetalol (Trandate, Normodyne): combined alpha/beta blocker

- Metoprolol tartrate (Lopressor) and metoprolol succinate (Toprol-XL)

- Nadolol (Corgard)

- Nebivolol (Bystolic)

- Penbutolol sulfate (Levatol)

- Propranolol (Inderal)

- Sotalol (Betapace)

- HCTZ and bisoprolol (Ziac): beta blocker plus diuretic

❖ **ACE inhibitors:** work on the angiotensin hormone in the body that causes blood vessels to narrow. The angiotensin-converting enzyme (ACE) inhibitors decrease the production of angiotensin, which in turn helps lower blood pressure. Examples of ACE inhibitors include:

- Benazepril hydrochloride (Lotensin)

- Captopril (Capoten)

- Enalapril Maleate (Vasotec)

♦ Fosinopril sodium (Monopril)

♦ Lisinopril (Prinivil, Zestril)

♦ Moexipril (Univasc)

♦ Perindopril (Aceon)

♦ Quinapril hydrochloride (Accupril)

♦ Ramipril (Altace)

♦ Trandolapril (Mavik)

❖ **Angiotensin II Receptor blockers:** also work on the hormone angiotensin, which needs a place to bind in order to do its job of narrowing blood vessels. That's where angiotensin II receptor blockers come in. They prevent angiotensin from binding to receptors on the blood vessels and that helps lower blood pressure. Angiotensin II receptor blockers include:

♦ Azilsartan (Edarbi)

♦ Candesartan (Atacand)

♦ Eprosartan mesylate (Teveten)

♦ Irbesarten (Avapro)

♦ Losartan Potassium (Cozaar)

♦ Olmesartan (Benicar)

- Telmisartan (Micardis)

- Valsartan (Diovan)

It's highly unlikely you need blood pressure medicine but if for some reason you and your doctor do think you need it, Angiotensin II Receptor blockers have a very small edge over the others because these can lower internal inflammation.

❖ **Calcium channel blockers:** Calcium increases the strength and force of contractions in the heart and blood vessels (calcium is good for you). Blocking its entry into smooth muscle tissue reduces this effect. Calcium channel blockers lower blood pressure by relaxing blood vessels and reducing heart rate. Examples of calcium channel blockers include:

- Amlodipine besylate (Norvasc, Lotrel)

- Clevidipine (Cleviprex)

- Diltiazem hydrochloride (Cardizem CD, Cardizem SR, Dilacor XR, Tiazac)

- Felodipine (Plendil)

- Isradipine (DynaCirc, DynaCirc CR)

- Nicardipine (Cardene SR)

- Nifedipine (Adalat CC, Procardia XL)

- Nimodipine (Nimotop, Nymalize)

- Nisoldipine (Sular)

- Verapamil hydrochloride (Calan SR, Isoptin SR, Verelan, Covera HS)

❖ **Alpha blockers:** cause blood vessels to dilate, thereby lowering blood pressure. These medications are also used to treat prostate enlargement in men. Alpha blockers include:

- Doxazosin mesylate (Cardura)

- Prazosin hydrochloride (Minipress)

- Terazosin hydrochloride (Hytrin)

❖ **Alpha-2 Receptor agonist:** Methyldopa, formerly known under the brand name Aldomet, is one of the oldest blood pressure medications still in use. It was first introduced more than 50 years ago. Methyldopa works on the central nervous system to lower blood pressure. While its general use has declined over the years, methyldopa is considered the first line of treatment for high blood pressure that develops during pregnancy.

❖ **Central agonists:** another group of hypertension medications that work on the central nervous system rather than directly on the cardiovascular system. Central agonists have a tendency to cause drowsiness. Drugs in this class include:

♦ Clonidine hydrochloride (Catapres)

♦ Guanfacine hydrochloride (Tenex)

❖ **Peripheral adrenergic inhibitors:** There was a time when the list of high blood pressure medications was very short indeed. In the 1950s, Reserpine (a peripheral adrenergic inhibitor) was one of the few products on the market to treat hypertension.

Today, it is rarely used due to its numerous side effects and drug interactions. Peripheral adrenergic inhibitors work in the brain to block signals that tell blood vessels to constrict. They are generally only used when other high blood pressure medications fail to solve the problem. Peripheral adrenergic inhibitors include:

♦ Guanadrel (Hylorel)

♦ Guanethidine monosulfate (Ismelin)

♦ Reserpine (Serpasil)

❖ **Vasodilators:** relax artery wall muscles to cause blood pressure to drop. These drugs are usually used in combination with others. They include:

♦ Minoxidil (Loniten): used only for severe hypertension

♦ Hydralazine (Apresoline)

♦ Minoxidil (Loniten)

The Cost of Heart Disease Treatment

WOW! That's an incredible list of heart disease medicines and it's probably not a comprehensive list. If it is currently comprehensive, just give it a month and it won't be.

You might be wondering why so many types and brands of medicines are developed, promoted, and distributed for this single health ailment. Begin by thinking **BIG MONEY**. It's almost certain that no one knows the total cost of these drugs. When you add on the associated costs of ambulances, hospital stays, doctors, surgery, etc., it has to be astronomical.

An April 2016 report in *American Health & Drug Benefits* found that the high costs associated with heart failure made up an estimated 23% of US hospital inpatient costs in a single year. But, as patients with the condition know, the cost of daily medications can add up substantially over a lifetime after they're discharged from the hospital.

Today, it's estimated that cardiovascular disease costs Americans $320 billion each year. But don't take that number at face value, because many heart treatment drugs are designed to be taken for the rest of your life. By 2030, annual direct medical costs associated with cardiovascular diseases are projected to rise to more than $818 billion!

Praluent is a new drug on the market, targeted at treating stubbornly high cholesterol. The manufacturer is asking $14,600 a year for injections.

The drug maker Novartis recently set a price of $4,560 a year for its new heart failure pill Entresto, nearly 50% higher than what many analysts had expected.

Praluent and its competitor Repatha are expected to generate global annual sales of more than $2 billion each in 2020, according to consensus forecasts compiled by Thomson Reuters Cortellis.

"Entresto is forecast to sell nearly $5 billion by the same date, a figure that has been steadily climbing since the price was set."

What are the most common blood pressure medications? In terms of dollar sales, recent statistics put the angiotensin II receptor blocker valsartan (Diovan) in the lead for high blood pressure medications, followed by the beta blocker metoprolol, the generic combination of valsartan and HCTZ, olmesartan (Benicar), and olmesartan and HCTZ (Benicar HCT).

High Blood Pressure Medicine Side Effects

Oh boy... Where to begin? Because of all the different high blood pressure drugs available, the possible interaction side effects are almost innumerable. It's highly unlikely any person or any one organization is aware of all of them. Here, we look at some that readers are most likely to encounter.

Any medication can have side effects. However, as stronger and stronger medicines come onto the market, the frequency and severity of side effects continue to increase. Blood pressure medicines are no different.

This does not mean that you will definitely have side effects from your medicines. There is usually no way to know ahead of time. If you do experience side effects, you will usually notice them soon after starting a new medicine, or after the amount of your dose is increased.

Just as not all people experience side effects, different individuals suffer different side effects from the same medication. For example, some people taking ACE inhibitors may develop a dry cough. Others taking the same medicine may have no cough but feel dizzy or have an upset stomach.

Medicines with known side effects come with information pamphlets listing those known side effects. Don't be surprised how long these lists are. Fortunately, no one person is likely to ever experience all of the side effects listed, though it's not unusual to have several of them.

Be fully aware that heart medicines (and other medicines) often interact with each other. These interactions are not limited to other prescription medicines. They can and do include herbal medicines as well as over-the-counter medicines such as cold remedies. If you choose to take prescribed medicines or any other medicines, **it's always best making sure your medical professional is aware of ALL of the medicines you are taking.**

SOME possible side effects of high blood pressure medicines include:

❖ Chest pain, heart palpitations (the feeling that your heart is racing), or arrhythmia (irregular heartbeat)

❖ Cough, fever, congestion, upper respiratory tract infection, or flu-like symptoms

❖ Diarrhea or constipation

- ❖ Dizziness or lightheadedness

- ❖ Headache

- ❖ Nausea

- ❖ Vomiting

- ❖ Nervousness or increased anxiety

- ❖ Problems with erection and sexual function

- ❖ Skin rash

- ❖ Tiredness, weakness, drowsiness, or lethargy (lack of energy)

- ❖ Unintended weight loss or gain

Some or possibly most of these might not sound too bad on a stand-alone basis. However, consider that you may well be taking these drugs for the rest of your life. Would you want to endure perpetual vomiting, skin rashes, or uncontrolled weight gain for the remainder of your life? And maybe all of them at the same time?

One side effect of diuretics (often a starter med for high blood pressure) is a loss of potassium, which is carried out of the body in urine along with sodium. Potassium is needed for proper muscular movement, and a deficiency of this mineral may result in fatigue, weakness, leg cramps, and even heart problems. Often, patients prescribed traditional diuretics will be advised to take their medication with a potassium-rich food such as orange juice or a banana, or they'll be prescribed a potassium supplement.

If I were you, I'd be very concerned with side effects and drug interactions. Fortunately, there are alternatives. Keep reading this entire book to learn what you probably would prefer to be doing to control high blood pressure and almost all other modern health ailments <u>for which internal inflammation is the root cause</u>.

But first...

High Blood Pressure Medication and ED

As research continues, more and more links between high blood pressure and ED are revealed. A recent study by researchers at the Department of Physiology, Georgia Health Sciences University, in Augusta, Georgia found that approximately 30% of men with hypertension complain of erectile dysfunction. High blood pressure isn't your only risk factor for ED though. Medications used to treat hypertension can also contribute to erectile dysfunction.

It's easy to understand: High blood pressure damages the arteries, and proper blood flow through those arteries is needed to obtain and maintain an erection.

Over time, hypertension can cause the arteries to become less flexible and narrower (atherosclerosis), resulting in reduced blood flow. This not only puts you at risk of heart attack and stroke, but it also limits the amount of blood that circulates to the penis and thereby decreasing your ability to achieve and sustain erections. High blood pressure can also impact libido and ejaculation.

It is a bit of a vicious circle, in that hypertension can cause ED if left untreated, but the medications used to treat hypertension can also impair sexual function and cause ED. Here is a partial list of high blood pressure medications known to cause erectile dysfunction as a side effect:

❖ **Beta blockers:** These affect the same part of the nervous system that is responsible for causing erections.

❖ **Diuretics:** Also referred to as "water pills," these can interfere with the intensity of blood flow to the penis making it difficult to achieve an erection. Diuretics are also known to lower zinc levels, which may interfere with the body's production of testosterone.

Other Serious Medical Issues We Are Misguided About

Making healthier lifestyle choices could **lower your blood pressure without the use of medication** and help you get your sex life back on track. And the list of bad medical issues goes on...

The List of Serious Medical Issues We've Been Misguided About Goes On and On

Now, that you're becoming aware that medical treatments such as overpowering medications, chemo, radiation, surgery, and other modern "cures" often bring on more problems than they fix, it's time to take a look at still more potentially damaging treatments.

Always keep in mind that I'm not a doctor, and I obviously don't know your medical situation. My intention is only to bring your attention to the many serious consequences of today's "miracle cures" and make you aware of alternatives that very likely will make you a whole man again — a man who doesn't need to suffer from all of the side effects that so many have relinquished their lives too.

Let's take a look at other serious medical issues you need to be aware of...

Know Your Cholesterol

This quote is straight from the website of the American Heart Association:

> "Although it is not proven that inflammation causes cardiovascular disease, inflammation

is common for heart disease and stroke patients and is thought to be a sign or atherogenic response. It's important to know what inflammation is and what it can do to your heart."

It's great that the medical community is slowly beginning to acknowledge that inflammation is at the root of many — or most, or even all — modern diseases. However, keep in mind that, for huge organizations with a financial interest in modern medicine, internal inflammation and leaky gut are only "suspect" at this time. Inflammation is not recognized as an official diagnoses — YET. That means internal inflammation is getting little or no attention in medical schools and medical literature.

While some researchers are beginning to take a closer look at this root problem, most of the medical community continues turning a blind eye to the problem, and the topic is not likely to make it into the mainstream conversation for a few more decades.

There are many misconceptions about the relationship between cholesterol and health. Are your afraid of having high cholesterol? Don't be. Do you throw away the egg yolks and only eat the whites? That's not helping your health. Are you taking cholesterol-lowering medicine or considering it? Read this first.

Uffe Ravnskov, MD, PhD, author of *The Cholesterol Myths: Exposing the Fallacy that Saturated Fat and Cholesterol Cause Heart Disease*, may be the world's leading expert on the relationship between cholesterol and human health. Here are some facts from his book that everyone concerned about cholesterol should know:

❖ **Cholesterol is NOT a deadly poison.** It's a substance you need to be healthy. High cholesterol itself does not cause heart disease.

❖ People who have low blood cholesterol have the same rates of heart disease as people who have high blood cholesterol.

❖ The cholesterol found in your blood comes from two sources: cholesterol in food that you eat and <u>cholesterol that your liver makes</u> from other nutrients. (Yep, your body actually makes its own cholersterol.)

The amount of cholesterol that your liver produces varies according to how much cholesterol you get from food. If you consume a lot of cholesterol, your liver produces less. If you don't consume much cholesterol, your liver produces more. This is why a low cholesterol diet does not typically decrease a

person's blood cholesterol by more than a few
percentage points.

❖ Drugs intended solely for lowering your
cholesterol do not decrease your risk of dying
from heart disease, nor do they increase your
lifespan. On the contrary, **these drugs pose
serious dangers to your health and will
probably decrease your life span.**

❖ The newer cholesterol-lowering drugs — called
statins — do reduce your risk of heart disease,
but they do it through mechanisms that are not
related to lowering blood cholesterol. And
alarmingly, statins like Lipitor, Mevacor, Zocor,
Pravachol, and Lescol are known to stimulate
cancer in rodents. Statins also cause type 2
diabetes and other serious health problems.
Much more to come about how bad statins are
for you.

About LDL and HDL

Some facts about LDL and HDL that the vast
majority of people are surprised to learn:

❖ LDL stands for low-density lipoprotein and HDL
stands for high-density lipoprotein.

❖ LDL and HDL are **NOT** types of cholesterol.

❖ LDL and HDL are lipoproteins that **transport
cholesterol** through your blood circulatory
system.

❖ LDL is often mistakenly thought of as "bad
cholesterol" because it carries cholesterol to
your arteries.

❖ HDL is often mistakenly referred to as "good
cholesterol" because it carries cholesterol away
from your arteries (to your liver).

❖ **LDL and HDL carry the same cholesterol.**

It's How Foods are Processed That Matters — Not Cholesterol

Cholesterol that naturally occurs in animal meats
and other food sources is not harmful to your
health. However, it can become **harmful to your
health when it is damaged by exposure to high
levels of heat and/or harsh processing
techniques.** High heat and harsh processing
techniques are most common in processed foods
and restaurants meals (restaurants cook at high
heat to get food to your table fast and hot).

If you regularly consume **damaged cholesterol** and
foods that are high in free radicals, you probably
have significant quantities of damaged cholesterol

circulating through your system.

And if you regularly have **damaged cholesterol** floating around in your blood, then a high LDL level (LDL carries cholesterol to your arteries) correlates with a higher-than-average risk of developing cardiovascular disease while a high HDL level (HDL carries cholesterol away from your arteries to your liver) correlates with a lower-than-average risk of developing cardiovascular disease.

In other words, if you have significant amounts of damaged cholesterol in your circulatory system, you don't want a lot of LDL available to carry this cholesterol to your arteries where the damaged cholesterol can contribute to atherosclerosis. But you do want a lot of HDL available to shuttle the damaged cholesterol away from your arteries.

Therefore, while it's true that a high HDL/total cholesterol ratio can reflect a lower risk of developing cardiovascular disease, what's most important when it comes to cholesterol and your health is that you avoid eating processed foods and foods that have been cooked at high temperatures, since these foods are typically rich in damaged cholesterol.

Your Cholesterol Should Be High

Not surprisingly, the guidelines promoting lower cholesterol are heavily driven by pharmaceutical companies that rake in billions of dollars with their cholesterol-lowering drugs. A blatant example is when a panel of physicians in 2004 lowered the "safe" level of LDL cholesterol from 130 to 100, and further recommended that people at high risk of developing cardiovascular disease aim to lower their LDL levels to 70.

I'm sure you can guess why this was done. This modification in one medical standard converted an estimated eight million Americans into instant candidates for cholesterol-related drug therapy. A wide swathe of the news media covered this changed medical standard without further research.

Only Newsday reported that <u>most of the physicians responsible for establishing the new recommendations had a conflict of interest</u>. Almost all of them had received money — usually in the form of grants or honoraria — from at least ten drug companies. The National Cholesterol Educational Program, the source of the new medical treatment guidelines for cholesterol, failed to disclose these financial dealings.

The truth is:

❖ Your cholesterol should be on the higher side

rather than the lower side (lower is
recommended to push more drugs). If you have
high cholesterol that you are concerned about,
the best natural treatment is raising your thyroid
and boosting your metabolism.

❖ It's best to have a blood cholesterol level of
above 150 mg/dL (3.9 mmol/L). But a blood
cholesterol level lower than this is not likely a
cause for concern, so long as you are eating a
nutrient-dense, protein/plant centered diet, and
not suffering from any health challenges.

❖ Low cholesterol over the long term has negative
repercussions. It may lead to depression,
increased risk of stroke, and multiple problems
related to hormonal imbalances. If you are not
getting enough vitamin D from your diet, low
cholesterol may lead to vitamin D deficiency
because <u>sunlight has to act on cholesterol found
in your skin to create vitamin D in your body</u>.

❖ Ideally, your HDL/total cholesterol ratio should
be above 25%. Generally, the higher this ratio,
the better. If this ratio is 10%-15% or lower,
there is increased risk of eventually experiencing
a heart attack.

❖ Ideally, it's best to have a triglyceride/HDL ratio
of 2.0 or lower.

❖ If your HDL/total cholesterol and triglyceride/HDL ratios are in the ranges listed above, and the cholesterol you consume is mainly undamaged cholesterol, a total cholesterol of more than 200 mg/dL (5.2 mmol/L) probably isn't a cause for worry. In fact, even people whose total cholesterol is above 350 mg/dL (9.0 mmol/L) because of genetics have been shown to have no elevated risk of heart disease as long as their ratios are fine and they stay away from eating damaged cholesterol.

Cholesterol builds up as a defense mechanism when you are not healthy. When you are healthy, the cholesterol converts into very desirable downstream steroid hormones. You want adequate cholesterol to support testosterone, DHT, progesterone, etc. When these hormone levels are healthy, your cholesterol level will drop if you don't get enough. Then your steroid hormone levels drop to unhealthy levels.

Dangers of Statins

Why are so many people being prescribed and taking statin drugs when these are plainly harmful to the human body in many ways? Statin cholesterol-lowering drugs are widely touted as the best way to lower your cholesterol and thereby prevent a heart attack. These are recommended for people who have "high cholesterol," those with heart disease, and even for some healthy people as a form of preventive medicine.

Statins are among the most widely-prescribed drugs on the market, with more than one in four Americans over the age of 45 taking them. This already large number is set to increase significantly due to draft recommendations issued in 2016 by the US Preventive Services Task Force (USPSTF).

This federal advisory board recommended statin treatment for people between the ages of 40 and 75 who have a 10% or greater risk of heart problems in the next 10 years (based on the 2013 AHA-ACC online calculator) — even if they have **not** previously had a heart attack or stroke.

Statins don't work. They do lower cholesterol, and as your levels fall, you might take that as proof that you're getting healthier and reducing your risk of heart disease and heart attack. But that would be far from the truth.

There is far more that goes into your risk of heart disease than your cholesterol levels. Further, there is evidence that shows that **statins may actually worsen your heart health** and only appear to be effective due to deception by statistics.

One report published in the Expert Review of Clinical Pharmacology concluded that statin advocates used a statistical tool called relative risk reduction (RRR) to amplify what are actually the trivial beneficial effects of statins.

If you look at **absolute risk**, using statin drugs benefits just 1% of the population. This means that out of 100 people treated with the drugs, 1 person will have 1 less heart attack. This doesn't sound very impressive so statin supporters use the "better" statistic of relative risk.

Just by using this statistical sleight of hand, statins suddenly appear to be beneficial for 30%-50% of the population. As the Statistics Department at George Mason University explains, "An important feature of relative risk is that **it tells you nothing about the actual risk.**"

Statins interfere with healthy bodily functions. Statins rob your body of the coenzyme Q10 (CoQ10), and this accounts for many of statin's devastating results. Although it was proposed to add a Black Box Warning to statins stating this, the US Food and Drug Administration (FDA) decided against it in 2014.

CoQ10 is used by every cell in your body for energy production, and is therefore vital for good health, high energy levels, longevity, and general quality of life. CoQ10's reduced form, ubiquinol, is a critical component of cellular respiration and production of adenosine triphosphate (ATP).

ATP is a coenzyme used as <u>an energy carrier by all of the cells in your body</u>. When you consider that your heart is your most energy-demanding organ, you can surmise how potentially devastating it can be to deplete your body's main source of cellular energy.

So, while one of statins' claims to fame is warding off heart disease, users are actually **increasing their risk** by depleting their bodies of CoQ10.

In March 2015, research published in *Expert Review of Clinical Pharmacology* revealed that, contrary to the current belief that cholesterol reduction via statins decreases atherosclerosis, the drugs may instead actually provoke atherosclerosis and heart failure.

The same study discussed several physiological mechanisms that show how statin drugs may make your heart health worse. One of those is that they inhibit the synthesis of vitamin K2 — vitamin K2 protects your arteries from calcification. Without it, plaque levels worsen.

Vitamin K2's biological role is to help move

calcium into the areas of your body that need it, such as your bones and teeth. It also plays a role in removing calcium from areas where it causes harm, such as your arteries and soft tissues.

A K2 deficiency can lead to other unwanted health conditions including:

❖ Osteoporosis

❖ Cancer

❖ Heart attack and stroke

❖ Inappropriate calcification, from heel spurs to kidney stones

❖ Heart disease

❖ Brain disease

Statins inhibit ketone production. Statins lower cholesterol by inhibiting the enzyme in your liver that produces cholesterol (HMG coenzyme A reductase). Unfortunately, this is the same enzyme that produces not only CoQ10, but also ketones, which are crucial nutrients for your mitochondria (these act like a digestive system, which takes in nutrients, breaks them down, and creates energy-rich molecules for cells). Ketones are indispensable biological signaling molecules.

Ketones are produced in your liver as byproducts of the breakdown of fatty acids, and production increases during fasting. As noted in the journal

Trends in Endocrinology & Metabolism:

> *"Ketone bodies are emerging as crucial
> regulators of metabolic health and longevity,
> via their ability to regulate HDAC (histone
> deacetylases) activity and thereby epigenetic
> gene regulation."*

Ketone bodies appear to inhibit HDAC function,
which is implicated in the regulation of aging.

Further, researchers noted:

> *"Ketone bodies may link environmental cues
> such as diet to the regulation of aging."*

This is not a bodily function that you want to turn
off or turn down.

Statins Increase Risk of Serious Diseases

As a result of statins depleting your body of CoQ10,
inhibiting synthesis of vitamin K2, and reducing the
production of ketone bodies, statin use increases
your risk of serious conditions, including:

❖ **Cancer:** Studies have found that extended use
of statins significantly increases the chance of
developing prostate cancer. In women, taking
statins for 10 years or more, increases the risk
of breast cancer two-fold.

❖ **Diabetes:** Statins have also been shown to

increase your risk of diabetes via a number of different mechanisms. The most important one is that they increase insulin resistance, which can be extremely harmful to your health. Secondly, statins increase your diabetes risk by raising your blood sugar (while giving almost no actual protection from death and these do increase sexual dysfunction). Remember, statins work by preventing your liver from making cholesterol. As a result, your liver returns sugar to your bloodstream, which raises your blood sugar levels. What's important is having proper balance between your blood sugar and cholesterol. If you have a family history of blood sugar problems or are pre-diabetic, you should talk to your doctor about the extra risk of statins and make clear your preference against taking them.

Statins also rob your body of certain valuable nutrients, which can also impact your blood sugar levels. Two nutrients in particular, vitamin D and CoQ10, are both needed to maintain ideal blood glucose levels.

❖ **Erectile dysfunction** is another terrible side effect of statins. **Cholesterol is the mother of all the steroid hormones.** It's the primary building block for everything, including the sex hormones. Estrogen, testosterone, DHT, cortisol,

and many others all start with cholesterol. **If you
lower your cholesterol, you're going to lower
the amount of sex hormones in your body.** The
study titled "Testicular Function in
Hypercholesterolemic Male Patients During
Prolonged Simvastatin Treatment" (published
2007) found testosterone levels declined quite a
bit and it was only due to the statin drug.

❖ **Cholesterol is also essential for your brain.**
Your brain contains about 25% of the cholesterol
in your body. It is critical for synapse formation.
Those are the connections between your
neurons that allow you to think, learn new
things, and form memories. It's not surprising
that memory loss is widely reported in
association with statin use.

Further, ketone bodies are used as fuel by your
brain, and have been demonstrated to protect
against neuronal disease, seizures, and age-
related brain diseases such as Alzheimer's,
Huntington's, and Parkinson's.

❖ Statin users are **more likely to suffer from
musculoskeletal conditions, injuries, and pain
than non-users.**

❖ Significantly more patients taking statins have
been found to develop cataracts than those not

taking the medication.

Everything considered, do you really want to take statins that reduce cholesterol (which should be high) but have shown no usefulness in reducing heart disease and heart attacks? **Please reconsider.**

Old Fashioned Heart Disease Treatments

Heart disease is sometimes called the "quintessential disease of civilization" because it was rare before 1900, and it remains much less common in pre-industrialized populations. In contrast, by the middle of the last century, coronary heart disease (CHD) became **the nation's biggest killer.**

Today all forms of cardiovascular diseases — including conditions of the heart and the blood vessels like angina, congestive heart failure, and stroke — are still the leading causes of death in many Western nations. Combined, all cardiovascular diseases kill more than one million Americans a year, men and women pretty much equally.

Don't you find it peculiar that, after 65-plus years of fighting the number one killer with modern "miracle" drugs, heart disease still remains the number one killer? Maybe, just maybe, these drugs are the wrong approach — **do you think?**

What's Really Causing Heart Disease and Heart Attacks

Calcium, cholesterol particles, and fatty acids accumulate on arterial walls and form a swelling called an atheroma. Atheromata are capable of bursting, causing blood clots, and leading to heart attacks or strokes. In populations that eat an **unprocessed diet**, far less inflammation-caused arteriosclerosis and heart disease is present.

Adjusting your diet, reducing stress levels, and staying active are fundamental to controlling inflammation and (therefore) naturally treating and preventing coronary heart disease. Many people are able to prevent coronary heart disease (CHD) and recover from it naturally by maintaining a healthy lifestyle: changing their diet, stopping smoking, getting quality sleep, using dietary supplements, and some other things we'll discuss later.

When most people think of foods that increase the potential for developing heart disease, fatty cuts of meat and fried foods probably come to mind. For many years, the public was led to believe that cholesterol-rich foods and saturated fats of all kinds increased the risk for developing coronary heart disease. "The cholesterol hypothesis" as it's called, rested on the assumption that saturated fats raise cholesterol and that cholesterol clogs arteries.

However, a number of researchers today have demonstrated that this is not necessarily true, and that while this theory has been widely accepted, it has never been proven. Cholesterol is actually an essential component of healthy cells and organisms, and we all need to maintain a certain level of it to thrive.

According to a 2009 study published in the *International Journal of Clinical Practice*, it is now acknowledged that the original studies purporting to show a linear relation between cholesterol intake and CHD may have contained fundamental design flaws, including merged cholesterol and saturated fat consumption rates and inaccurately assessed actual dietary intake of fats by study subjects.

<u>In the majority of people, the real cause of heart disease is internal inflammation.</u> Foods that promote inflammation the most include processed foods, corn/soybean/other vegetable oils, and trans fats.

In years gone by, skeptics of the cholesterol theory weren't exactly embraced by the medical community or the public. It was a hard sell, trying to tell people that they didn't need to worry about eating things like high-quality butter, beef, and eggs anymore. But it's becoming more accepted that these types of foods are not harmful for most people, and in fact are usually beneficial.

For most of the population, cholesterol screening tests can be misleading or even harmful, as they're now considered unlikely to reduce mortality risk.

Going Forward With a Healthy Heart

When it comes to saturated fats raising cholesterol, the topic needs some explaining. Saturated fat does raise cholesterol but not in what's considered an unhealthy or unsafe way for most people. Certain saturated fats, when compared with polyunsaturated fats, do usually raise total cholesterol levels in most people, but we now know that total cholesterol is a poor predictor of heart disease in general.

Saturated fats raise HDL cholesterol, commonly known as the "good cholesterol," while polyunsaturated fats lower this type — **low cholesterol is even worse than high**!

Despite the existing evidence that consuming cholesterol isn't the cause of heart disease, most government-funded health organizations, including the National Heart, Lung, and Blood Institute, still recommend limiting saturated fats. Going forward, we can expect guidelines like this to be updated to reflect the most recent study findings. Over the last decade, many other countries and health promotion groups have already modified their dietary recommendations to reflect the current evidence.

A warning about stents for a coronary artery (an artery feeding the heart muscle). Stents are almost always an unneeded medical procedure. The medical term for a stent procedure is Percutaneous Coronary Intervention (PCI). According to Harvard Medical School, "an estimated two million people get coronary artery stents every year, and if you have coronary artery disease, there is a good chance your doctor will suggest you get one." But this is being overly influenced by medical device makers (remember I'm not a doctor). The most common application is for <u>stable</u> coronary artery disease. In plain English, it usually means there is a heart artery blockage that is <u>producing no or very little symptoms</u>. A New England Journal of Medicine article (Optimal Medical Therapy with or without PCI for Stable Coronary Disease) found that *"Recent registry data indicate that approximately 85% of all PCI procedures are <u>undertaken electively</u> in patients with stable coronary artery disease."* The primary reason for the elective surgery is to make the patient feel better even when there is not a medical need. In fact, <u>stents do not save lives</u>. As the study puts it, *"As an initial management strategy in patients with stable coronary artery disease, PCI did not reduce the*

*risk of death, myocardial infarction, or other
major cardiovascular events when added to
optimal medical therapy."* They don't prolong
life. And they don't keep you from having a heart
attack either. What stents are is very expensive —
as well as extremely invasive. Shouldn't you
consider the many other options that don't involve
installing foreign objects next to your heart?

Radiation Cancer Therapy Today

Here is another medical issue that we've been
misguided about. Radiation consists of waves of
energy, such as light or heat. The form of radiation
used in cancer therapy is ionizing radiation — a
high-energy form of radiation. Scientists named it
"ionizing radiation" because it has enough energy to
remove electrons from atoms, thus forming ions.

Exactly how radiation works as a treatment for
cancer is complex and is still being researched. But
basically, it breaks up the DNA of cancer cells in
such a way as to disrupt their growth and division,
and even to kill them.

There are two types of radiation therapy:

❖ **External beam radiation therapy:** The beam of
   radiation is focused by an external machine onto
   the treatment area.

❖ **Internal radiation therapy (such as brachytherapy):** an internal radioactive substance is placed within or close to the cancerous tissue.

Brachytherapy is a recent development and is used in prostate cancer treatment and for other applications. This form of internal radiation therapy involves introducing low-energy radioactive metal that has a short effective range — it exerts its effects in a localized area to disrupt nearby cancer cells.

Highly radioactive material can be temporarily placed in or near the tissue — held in a tube for example — and then removed. Or less radioactive brachytherapy "seeds" can be left in place permanently with the radioactivity gradually dropping off. In between those two are a spectrum of brachytherapy delivery methods, there are also radioactive wires that may be left in place for a number of days.

As a newer cancer treatment, many of the risks remain unknown. Depending on the dose, or number of seeds, brachytherapy can cause a person to become mildly radioactive and some precaution may need to be exercised.

For pregnant women, safety is all about distance.

The List of Serious Medical Issues We've Been Misguided About Goes On and On

Pregnant women can safely be within three feet of a man with an actively-seeded prostate, but they should not sit next to, hug, or be intimate with a patient undergoing brachytherapy.

Additionally, it can be dangerous for prostate seed implantees to hold children on their laps. Because children under age 18 are particularly vulnerable to radiation-related problems, it is best to limit time with children to one hour per day at a three-foot distance during active treatment.

A month into treatment, the one-hour time limit can be reduced, but everyone should still abide by the three-foot rule while the seeds are active. Additionally, some men undergoing brachytherapy may be asked to avoid sex for the first two to four weeks of treatment.

For the men undergoing brachytherapy, the side effects are very similar to those caused by external beam radiation, and include irritation to the bladder, irritation of the rectum resulting in more frequent urination, more frequent bowel movements, tiredness, and long-term side effects including difficultly with erections. Additionally, based on such factors as your age and the age of your partner, for a period of time you may be asked to avoid embracing your partner from the back in the "spooning" position in bed.

Examples of acute or immediate side effects include:

- ❖ Local swelling.

- ❖ Local bruising.

- ❖ Semen may be discolored. In rare cases, it may contain expelled pellets and patients are therefore advised to use barrier contraception during sexual intercourse.

- ❖ Bleeding.

- ❖ Pain and discomfort at the site of the implant.

- ❖ General feeling of fatigue.

Some side effects occur within days or weeks of treatment and others may not appear for six or more months after treatment. Over time, you may notice that you are not having as many erections as you used to.

This is because the radiation from the seeds can harm the nerves near your prostate that help you have erections. This situation may or may not improve over time and happens to about half of the men who undergo brachytherapy.

Other General Cancer Treatment Risks

Of course, men are diagnosed with other types of

cancers that are accompanied by other treatment options and other risks. There are many more types of cancer than can be covered in this book. You should research your specific cancer (or other health condition) for a better understanding of it, its treatments, and associated side effects. What follows is general information about some other cancer treatments and risks.

All drugs used to treat cancer cause side effects. The side effects of each drug vary from individual to individual, though. Some people find that they only get very mild side effects. You may experience one, two, or more side effects from a particular drug.

It is not possible to say beforehand whether you should expect a particular side effect, when the effect will start or stop, or how bad it will be for you. These issues depend on many factors including:

❖ Which drugs you are taking.

❖ How long you have been taking the drugs.

❖ Your general health.

❖ The dosage.

❖ The way the drug is administered (for example, as a tablet or injection).

❖ Other drugs or cancer treatments that you are
taking.

❖ Some side effects are serious medical conditions
in their own right and will also need to be
treated.

❖ Some side effects, while inconvenient or
upsetting, are not harmful to your health.

The bottom line is that cancers are being over-
treated at great risk to patients, thanks to side
effects.

This section of the book does not attempt to cover
cancers in depth. I've discussed prostate cancer
statistics, treatments, and side effects in depth and
given you some general information on the side
effects of cancer treatment.

By now, you should be coming to understand that
modern medicine is not a cure-all and brings on
more problems than it actually solves. While most
of the side effects of medical treatment may not be
life-threatening, you certainly want to closely
consider quality of life issues before submitting
your body to most of these treatments and
medicines.

Diabetes is Naturally Treatable
If diabetes is a problem that you have, you are

almost certainly frustrated and scared about what you have been told. Yes, it can lead to ED, heart disease, strokes, blindness, amputations, and many other horrible side effects.

First, here are some facts that, though they seem kind of dramatic, you absolutely need to know about them because they reveal more about why you need to cure your diabetes than anything else I know of.

Diabetes is a plague. Here's some 2014 data from the Center for Disease Control:

❖ 29.1 million people (9.3% of the population) have diabetes.

❖ 21 million of those have been diagnosed.

❖ 8.1 million people (27.8%) with diabetes are undiagnosed.

❖ 86 million people have pre-diabetes (9 out of 10 don't know this about themselves).

That's just in America. It's getting worse all over the world with the spread of **SAD — the Standard American Diet**.

The most shocking part of this story is that it's totally preventable, reversible, and curable. That's

the good news — you can be cured of diabetes and
the root causes naturally, using home remedies.

You might be the victim of a lot of misinformation.
If you are frustrated with your diabetes diagnosis, if
you're tired of sticking yourself with needles, if
you're tired of taking expensive and dangerous
drugs, if you're sick to death of eating, bland,
tasteless, boring food — all while seeing no results
— you're going to want to hear what I have to say.

What you need is a natural remedy. You don't need
to be taking insulin, sticking yourself with needles,
and you definitely don't need to take even more
dangerous medications that destroy your body's
natural healing response system.

Here are a few basic rules that you'll need to follow
to begin bringing your blood sugars down toward
the normal range.

❖ Begin by eliminating foods containing artificial
   sweeteners from your diet. This doesn't just
   mean eliminating artificially sweetened candies
   and soda pops. It includes many starchy foods
   like breads, pastas, and most grains. There are
   some starches you'll be able to eat regularly
   such as white potatoes and well-cooked white
   rice. When you eat starches, drink some orange
   juice for the fructose that will counter balance

the glucose. Avoid brown rice because of the toxins in the husk.

❖ Sugar is good as the primary source of carbohydrates if you eat a good diet with plenty of fruit, protein, calcium, etc. Most sugar should come from fruit and juice. You can even drink full sugar soda pop, but not artificially sweetened.

But not everyone is the same and some people do not do well on high sugar diets. These seem to be people with low metabolism. Those that don't do well with sugar should eat more starches like well-cooked potatoes and well-cooked white rice.

Some people do okay on wheat and if so, sourdough white bread is best, Italian pastas (made with semolina flour from Italy seems much better than bread made in America) and others. Ideally, bread should be made with a long slow soak to lower gluten. Sprouted grains are even better and are available.

Watch iron because it is often added to bread and is very, very toxic by creating free radicals, lipofuscin, and interacting with PUFAs to create massive poisons.

❖ Carbs are good for you. But if you are working to overcome diabetes, you may need to monitor

153

your total carbohydrate intake to an amount that works with your injected insulin or your body's remaining phase 2 insulin output, if there is any. This would be a carbohydrate level that doesn't cause your blood sugars to rise above the narrow range of 75-90 mg/dl. This is to prevent overworking any functioning beta cells in your pancreas.

❖ Stop eating when you no longer feel hungry. There's no reason to clean your plate or eat until you're stuffed. Most diabetics need to lose weight.

❖ Keep the amount of food you eat consistent from one day to the next. This includes the fats and proteins if you are already eating a diet balanced with carbohydrates. Eating the right foods frequently lowers free fatty acids and helps the body heal from type 2 diabetes. This is important for diabetics taking injections or blood sugar reducing medicines. Under-eating can result in severe hypoglycemia.

I'm not going into all of the hassles and dangers associated with medical diabetes treatments here. You probably know as well anyone that it starts with pills that typically stop working at some point and then progresses to insulin injections. None of it is fun and none of it is healthy for you.

You only need to focus on three things. First, you absolutely need to know about the one thing you must avoid if you want to cure your diabetes. Actually, this is not really going to surprise you. Improve your diet by eliminating foods with artificial sweeteners. Avoid <u>ALL</u> artificial sweeteners, breads, and most white stuff (bleached food).

You must cut out the obvious stuff like artificially sweetened ice cream and diet soda (full sugar soda is fine). Just doing this one thing will help you begin to lower your blood sugar quickly and easily. These are good carbs that you should include: potatoes, yams, honey, orange juice, and other natural sugars.

This definitely is not the Big Pharma approach that can harm your body forever.

The "low insulin" theory of diabetes is not correct at all.

It's all about sugars and starches, small amounts of GOOD fats, and moderate protein intake, and avoiding food toxins.

You do NOT have to go ultra-low carb to cure type 2. In fact, HIGH carb works better. Fats cause insulin resistance, but carbs (including sugar) do not.

155

Here is a summary:

1. Go for high carb — starches that are safe in moderation include well-cooked potatoes, white rice, yams, sweet potatoes, carrots, turnips, and beets (again, all in moderation). All should be WELL cooked.

2. Go super low fat and only safe fats (no PUFA fats) — grass-fed butter, coconut oil, fat from lamb or beef. Good fats = saturated fats such as those from grass-fed animals, coconut oil, olive oil (in moderation and always uncooked), and wild fish (not fish oil and no oily fish, no sardines or salmon).

   Bad fats = ALL seed oils and PUFAs (much more on this to come), which can CAUSE diabetes on their own! Avoid ALL seed oils (corn, soy, safflower). Olive oil in moderation (always uncooked and no more than a teaspoon per day because it has moderate omega 6, not high but not terribly low).

3. Moderate chicken intake — once a week or less. Only white meat chicken, boneless and skinless chicken breasts that don't contain omega-6. Be aware that chicken is not your best choice as a protein source. Other parts of the chicken can be eaten less frequently but only occasionally. The other parts contain some omega-6 but not

enough to cause problems if eaten less often.
Breasts are preferred. But NO chicken fat.

4. Avoid food toxins — "fake" foods or processed
   foods, grains (except white rice), beans,
   especially soy products, and all sugar substitutes
   (no exceptions).

5. Moderate protein intake — not TOO much, no
   HUGE steaks (you want portions the size of a
   deck of playing cards). Too much protein
   triggers a metabolic equivalent of too many
   carbs, AND activates the mTOR pathway that
   increases the risk of cancer, inflammation, etc.

   Meats (and grains) have a down side by having
   too much phosphorous. <u>You need to offset
   phosphorous with more calcium.</u> High
   phosphorus combined with low calcium increases
   production of parathyroid hormone (PTR) and
   this pulls calcium out of the bones, hardening
   the arteries, calcifying the heart valve and
   kidneys, and ruining the testes and penis' ability
   to get erections. A good source of calcium is
   leafy greens (where cows get it).

6. Gentle and healthy cooking — steaming or
   boiling, as opposed to high temperature sautéing
   and roasting. High temperatures are okay
   occasionally but not all the time (one of the big
   reasons restaurant food is bad for you is the high

heat the chefs use to cook the food more quickly).

And sugar, of course. You need to become good at reading and interpreting ingredient labels on foods. U.S. food laws allow manufacturers to substitute any number of other sugars for sucrose and still call the product sugar-free.

It's important to note that sucrose is okay — sucrose, or table sugar, is a balanced sugar).

Sugars don't usually increase your blood sugar levels.

For the most part, they are safe to consume, even for diabetics.

Of course, always monitor your sugar levels and consult with your doctor.

Natural sugars include:

- ❖ Honey
- ❖ Maple syrup
- ❖ Fructose
- ❖ Glucose
- ❖ Dextrose (same as glucose)
- ❖ Molasses
- ❖ Table sugar

Remember, ALL artificial sweeteners out there are bad for a diabetic to eat.

Some people try to make an exception for stevia. This is a mistake. Stevia also needs to be avoided.

There are a few sweet food products that really are sugar-free, but there are very few. And **most of those contain toxins that are bad for you** and your diabetes. Sugar-free sodas are a big problem for diabetics. For the most part, all contain toxic artificial sweeteners.

You can use the list of sugars above to check ingredient lists. However, food manufacturers are constantly coming up with new artificial ingredients and previously unused sources of sugar — meaning that list will soon be out of date. The basic solution is to be very skeptical and avoid anything marketed as "artificially sweetened" or "sugar-free."

For example, sugar-free Jell-O brand ready-to-eat gelatin is free of sugar, but the powdered version is not. And DaVinci brand sugar-free syrups will work. There are new products coming on the market constantly, and I'm sure you'll find others to satisfy your sweet tooth without causing your blood sugars to get out of control.

Most diabetics are able to eat a normal diet that is high in carbohydrates, high in sugar, and low in fat.

You should be getting most calories from carbohydrates, not fat — about 70% of calories from carbs. And most carbs should be simple sugars, preferably those found in ripe fruit, orange juice, guava juice, and grape juice.

It's the same diet you need to eat to eliminate internal inflammation. Again, the big thing is avoiding processed foods, bad fats, and eating much fat in general.

When you consume sugar, quite often you're getting it in donuts, cakes, cookies, or other bakery products. These all contain large amounts of PUFAs (polyunsaturated fatty acids) such as vegetable oil, canola oil, soybean oil, and so on.

If you consume a lot of natural sugar through ripe fruit, good quality fruit juice, honey, etc., then this study indeed shows that you have nothing to worry about regarding weight gain: "Effect of Fructose on Body Weight in Controlled Feeding Trials: A Systematic Review and Meta-analysis." (You can find it in the Annals of Internal Medicine: http://annals.org/article.aspx?articleid=1132642.)

Diabetes and Erectile Dysfunction

Erectile dysfunction is often a serious problem for men with diabetes. It's estimated that about 75% of men with diabetes will have a problem with ED at some point in their lives. Men with diabetes tend to develop ED problems about ten to fifteen years younger than nondiabetics (both situations can be overcome). Above the age of 50, between 50% and 60% of men develop problems with diabetes. Above the age of 70, the percentage skyrockets to 95%.

The good news is that ED caused by diabetes is one of the most treatable symptoms of diabetes. In this book, we'll look at ways for you to regain your sexual health and control your diabetes.

ED is not just occasionally being unable to achieve and maintain an erection sufficient for intercourse. That happens to every man, and is typically caused by fatigue, illness, alcohol, drug use, or stress. It's not fun, but it does happen.

ED means frequently or never being able to achieve an erection sufficient for intercourse. Men with diabetes often also have a lower sex drive brought on by lowered testosterone levels, other hormone imbalances, and/or depression.

Just because type 2 diabetes and ED are both associated with age doesn't mean either or both are caused by aging. A man of any age that is mentally and physically healthy should be able to have an erection. Age has nothing to do with it.

Here is how diabetes can bring on ED. Achieving and maintaining an erection is a relatively complicated physiological process requiring the coordination of nerves, blood vessels, hormones, and psyche (libido). When any one of these is out of tune, ED can set in. Diabetes can affect any one or all of these physiological and mental processes.

Depression brought on by the diagnoses of diabetes can affect the psychological ability to obtain an erection. In addition, diabetes is well known for damaging blood vessels and nerves, which can affect the physical ability to obtain an erection.

A proper diet has been shown to reverse much of the damage that diabetes has already done, so don't panic yet. We will get to much more natural and healthy solutions before this book is over. But first consider...

ED Treatments That DO and DON'T Work

Fallacies of ED Medical Treatments

Erectile dysfunction brings on many problems both in the bedroom and outside of it. My definition of ED includes the obvious: not being able to get hard at the appropriate time. And it goes on to include going soft while having sex of all types.

Oh, and there's also premature ejaculation — and the other side of that coin: when you pump and pump away without being able to come. All of these are signs of erectile dysfunction.

It's natural to have a hard-on most of the night. It's also natural to wake up with one in the morning. If you don't experience that most of the time, you almost certainly suffer from ED. **Regaining morning wood is also the first indication that you are recovering from ED.**

Another indication that you're suffering from ED includes when your penis isn't as sensitive as it used to be. You should become semi-hard when you kiss her or even when only thinking about her.

Other ED Indicators. Do you still find sex to be the most pleasurable sensation there is? You should at any age. Age doesn't have anything to do with having an active and fulfilling sex life.

Often, ED is a combination of more than one of the symptoms listed above. They often come in phases, with the ultimate result of not being able to get hard when you want to or at any time.

The root causes of almost all sexual dysfunction in men are either low testosterone levels (caused by bad diet/internal inflammation), or desensitization of Dr. Willey (your penis). What's even more shocking is that all of the crap you're being told to do to treat sexual dysfunction is almost certainly doing you more harm than good.

Yes, all of those expensive little pills, the penis pumps, the gels, and the injections are doing more harm than good. They work for a short time and then they stop working all together. Those are NOT your answers to enjoying sex every day for the rest of your life.

And then there is surgery. Do you really want a doctor to cut open that appendage and try to fix it? Ouch... NOT ME!

You're Not a Cowboy

It's a studied and well-known fact that men today have much lower testosterone levels than men of a generation or two ago. Today, few men ride the range herding cattle or go hunting for their daily food. Most men work comfortably inside air-conditioned buildings and avoid the harshness of

Mother Nature. When they get off work, they plop down in an easy chair, pop open a beer, and spend the evening in front of the TV.

Some of the theories that try to explain why men are less "manly" today include the modern economy, television, video games, and feminism. Some believe (not me) that T-levels drop naturally as men age. But if that were true, how can you explain why young men in their 20s now have about half the testosterone of young men their age in the recent past? The fact is that testosterone levels in today's men are much lower than they were in generations gone by.

One of the biggest causes of the significantly lower testosterone levels in most men today is the dramatic increase in estrogen that men are exposed to. Estrogen is the dominant sexual hormone in women. Men have it also, but it should be at much lower levels.

Chemically, estrogen cancels out and blocks the desired effects of testosterone in the male body (leading to decreased sex drive and performance). When you reduce the estrogen in your body, the effects of your naturally-occurring testosterone will increase and you'll be one step closer to enjoying sex every day for the rest of your life. Personally, I plan to be having sex well into my 90s and beyond.

Again, it's the ultra-modern lifestyle that is introducing all of the estrogens into your body. It comes from many of the household products that you use every day: You smear them on your skin and consume them in your food. Our forefathers never came into contact with such products.

There are other causes for lower testosterone levels in today's men. Most are also related to our modern lifestyle and can be naturally reversed so that you can and will enjoy sex every day for the rest of your life.

Why You Don't Want Big Pharma Solutions

I'm not interested in the pharmaceutical strong medicine solutions, so I haven't investigated how much profit they make selling their gels, pills, and injections. I'm sure it's way up in the billions and they aren't going to stop pushing their high-risk/limited-results solutions anytime soon.

Testosterone Replacement Therapy (TRT) is fraught with health risks, not only to the man undergoing the treatment, but to anyone he comes into physical contact with when using the gel version. Besides the gel version, there are several other versions including injections and pills. **None of them are without serious side effects.**

All of the side effects from TRT (especially the long-term side effects) are not yet known, but here is a partial list of what is known:

- ❖ Increased risk of heart attack.

- ❖ Sleep apnea.

- ❖ Acne.

- ❖ Male breast enlargement.

- ❖ Benign growths in the prostate or increased growth of existing cancer in the prostate.

- ❖ Lower sperm production and/or testicle shrinkage.

- ❖ Increased risk of deep-vein clotting.

- ❖ Swelling of appendages.

- ❖ Difficulty urinating and weak urine flow.

- ❖ Frequent urination and an urgent need to urinate.

- ❖ Waking at night with a need to urinate.

- ❖ Nausea.

- ❖ Vomiting.

- ❖ Yellowed or darkened skin.

If a woman or child comes into contact with testosterone gels, it can cause serious side effects in them, including unwanted hair growth and premature puberty.

Now, let's move on to the cause of another modern phenomenon that has destroyed the sex lives of many men: **desensitization...**

Desensitization Has Many Causes

Desensitization results in Dr. Willey either not performing or not enjoying the performance. The opposite of not being able to perform at all is getting hard but never coming or having an orgasm. Both result in sexual frustration and drastically reduce the quality of your sex life.

Do you view porn regularly? Or masturbate too often? Or masturbate to porn on a daily basis? Or use a death grip when masturbating? Those are all aspects of our modern society that can cause sexual desensitization.

Today's porn is very different from when Marilyn Monroe first appeared in Playboy Magazine as "Sweetheart of the Month" in December of 1953. Today, porn is part of everyday life. What you view online these days is known as hardcore porn and it's a major cause of desensitization.

Hardcore porn is far from a representation of healthy sex. It's actresses and actors preparing for and performing in scripted scenes. There's a director in the background giving instructions to do the scene over and over again so that it can be filmed from different angles. This is not natural sex. When you become re-sensitized, you'll again enjoy the pleasures your woman can give you.

Old-fashioned porn has become mainstream. At one time it was censured, but long-ago advertising executives learned that sex sells and they have been pushing the boundaries ever since. It appears every few minutes in TV commercials and constantly in TV shows. It's bigger than life on roadside billboards that today show moving digital images.

All of this constant exposure to sex creates an unrealistic expectation for your sexual psyche and results in desensitizing you sexually because you're exposed to it way too often.

You Can Overcome Desensitization

Desensitization is a physiological problem. Yes, it is in your head, but it's not a psychological problem. It's about the hormones and chemicals in your head. When you are over-exposed to sexual stimulation, too much dopamine is released into your head.

What you want is to have more oxytocin in your brain. Making this change requires a change in your behavior. The good news is there is an all-natural process that is much safer than the strong medicines pushed by the drug companies that can treat some of the symptoms but in no way offer a real cure.

Doctors, counselors, therapists, and other professionals just don't get it. They will tell you that it's a mental issue in your head. One of their favorite tropes is telling you that it is caused by stress. Another common explanation is anxiety. Sure, these can contribute to desensitization but they are not the main causes.

In fact, erectile dysfunction and other desensitization symptoms can actually bring on stress, anxiety, and depression. When you correct the root cause, these other symptoms will decrease or disappear.

Viagra wasn't even intended as a sex drug. The drug companies were researching a heart medication when they discovered the drug they were working on had the ability to give some men erections. They had also been researching other drugs intended to help with men's sexual problems. That research mostly stopped when they stumbled upon Viagra. From then on, the research focused mostly on Viagra-type drugs. Nothing is going on around the subject of desensitization.

Doctors are trained to evaluate symptoms and prescribe medications to relieve those symptoms. They don't have any training regarding what I am teaching about desensitization. In fact, I have doctors that are students of these techniques because they also suffer from desensitization themselves and can't cure themselves.

A doctor's other option for you is surgery. If prescribing a pill doesn't work, cut something out. What they don't do is recommend lifestyle changes that can make you healthy. In days gone by, doctors didn't have all the medications they have today, and they didn't have the surgery techniques that are now available. They had to take a closer look at people's lifestyles to try to determine a change that would help the man. As such, they were more likely to get down to the root cause.

Something else that's a result of desensitization is premature ejaculation (PE), the other side of the ED coin. I found that often when a guy I work with gets over his ED, he comes really fast for a short time until his brain and body get used to his new-found sensitivity and pleasure.

Fortunately, premature ejaculation is a temporary problem. Guys with PE problems who follow the Cook solution find they start lasting **a really long time** (30 minutes or more), and **experience incredible sensation and pleasure.** The PE disappears forever, never to happen again. You'll soon be enjoying long-lasting and highly pleasurable sex for the rest of your life.

Here's a summary of what you may be struggling with that can be easily overcome:

The Four ED Indicators Are:

❖ Trouble getting hard.

❖ Going soft during sex.

❖ Premature ejaculation.

❖ Delayed ejaculation.

Next, I want to share with you some ED myths and natural recovery solutions...

What a Natural ED Solution Does for You and Her

This is for guys looking for a natural solution to erectile dysfunction (or even occasional ED) that doesn't involve dangerous, expensive, and physically addictive drugs like Viagra and Cialis, or gels, painful testosterone shots, vacuum pumps, etc.

I spent years researching every medical and alternative treatment for ED you can think of, and I was almost ready to toss in the towel.

For the longest time, all I found is that Big Pharma drugs and severe medical treatments are not the answer you and I are looking for.

You should know that I do not sell herbs, potions, drugs, or supplements of any kind. I am just going to tell you why you want to first try a natural brew instead of poisonous chemical medications.

Do Yourself and Your Manhood a Favor

First, be warned that what I'll be sharing with you goes against almost everything you've ever heard about ED. If you've jumped ahead in this book, you may still think that ED is a mental thing or an age-related problem, or that you don't even have ED because you only occasionally lose your erections.

Perhaps you suffer from soft or incomplete erections. You know, those woodies that create the awkward "cram it in any way you can" moments that leave you humiliated as you watch your lover try to hide the disappointment.

Maybe you're suffering from temporary erections that wither away within a few seconds of engaging in sex. Those are worse than not getting it up in the first place. It's like giving your lover a present and then taking it away before she can open the box. Believe me, women remember those disappointments longer than you'd like to think.

Then there's what I call "sensationless sex." That's when you can get it up for a brief shot, but the sensation and pleasure you feel is a fraction of what it used to be like. Sensitivity is very important to you. **So take special note here, because you may not even realize that your penile sensation has all but vanished.**

Think back to when you were a teenager. Those times when you were sitting in math class or history class and the mere thought of seeing that cute blonde in her cheerleader outfit made you sprout wood — usually right before your teacher asked you to come to the front of the room and solve some equation or present your homework. Now, that's embarrassing, right?

I remember having to hide more than one untimely erection, and, if you're honest with yourself, you long for those days. I bet you could barely keep yourself from releasing too quickly when you did get to have sex. All of was due to your member's sensitive nerves always being on red alert. Keep reading, as I am going to reveal to you how you can get that sensitivity back.

Now, something tells me that you don't often (if ever) wake up these days with that infamous "morning wood" like you used to, either.

Does any of this sound familiar to you? As you'll soon learn, these are early warning signs. Even if these terrifying things have happened to you only a few times, the reality is very clear. You have been caught in the throes of early or mid-stage erectile dysfunction.

And that often leads to full blown ED which can leave you in a permanent and irreversible state of what's called penile tissue decay, or PTD (penis shrinkage). In fact, unless you handle your ED right now, you can lose up to one inch off your member every year.

-Or-

You could feel forced to resort to painful and risky surgeries where the doctor slices your penis open from the base to the head and then peels the head flap open, scrapes out the delicate, sensitive, spongy erectile tissue and replaces it with a balloon. This balloon is manually inflated by vigorously and repeatedly squeezing a third "testicle" sewn into your scrotum. If that isn't an early sexual grave, I don't know what is. Scary stuff!

So, if the condition persists, the worst thing that can happen to a man will happen to you. You will stop wanting to have sex. Even now, your drive to have sex is probably going downhill, heading for a complete loss of sexual motivation. When that happens, your brain signals your body that it's time to die.

That's not an exaggeration. Your body will start burning muscle tissue and storing more fat, and you will lose more hair. The reason is simple. Sex is the signal to your brain that you are a hunter, a warrior, a true man. Your body is programmed to begin shutting down your vital systems when you no longer want sex. Now, even if that were the only repercussion of ED, it would be a really good reason to panic. But that's not all that happens.

What Your ED Does to Your Woman
Through my years of exploring this subject, I discovered that the problem causes even more

problems than you think. In fact, it isn't just a male problem. Women suffer from ED as well. Not in the physical way that we do, mind you, but in the emotional and sexual sense.

If you think that you can coast along and just assume that your woman will stand by your side, think again. Women feel shame and embarrassment when their lovers can't maintain an erection, and they blame themselves. No matter what she tells you or how much you tell her it's not her fault, very likely she blames herself.

Think about it: If a woman said she wanted to have sex with you, said she loved you, said she thought you were attractive and desirable, but then her body betrayed her by literally shutting down sexually, what would you believe?

Single Men With ED

Now, what if you're single? Well then, I bet you're terrified of that first sexual encounter with the next girl you meet. The anxiety you must feel knowing there is a massive chance that your member will just sag in her hands or go totally limp and shrink after only a few minutes of sexual contact, well that's enough to overwhelm the strongest guy in the world.

Over 72% of single men over the age of 45 report a high degree of sexual anxiety when it comes to their first time with a new partner. When a man can't get it up, it leads to humiliation, rejection by his partner, and greater social isolation.

If you can't go into the bedroom confident that you can perform on command, you are setting yourself up for a vicious cycle of embarrassment and disappointment. But this doesn't have to happen.

Starting today, you can return to the time when a strong breeze would give you a rise in your jeans, when you could perform at a moment's notice, often for hours and multiple times in a row.

I believe that's the right of every man at any age!

Let's address the problem head on before things get out of hand.

ED Myths

During my years of suffering from ED and searching for natural ways to reverse it, I discovered three very common myths that most men believe when it comes to getting and keeping firm erections. I want to save you months and possibly years of frustrating searching — and a hell of a lot of money too — by exposing these myths and lies, right now.

The first myth is one that I heard all my life, and you've probably heard it as well. "It's all in your head." Well, guess what? It's all in your penis. That myth got started because men reported feeling anxious during sex, and the result of that was the cart being put before the horse. Anxiety became the "reason" for soft or nonexistent erections. **In reality, poor erections are the reason for the anxiety.**

Just think about it. When you were a teenager, did you feel anxious before sex? If you're honest with yourself, you certainly did. But you still got hard enough to drive a nail through a 4x4, didn't you? It's not in your head, at least not the head on your shoulders. You have a physical problem, and we're going to solve that problem shortly.

The second myth is one that can break you financially, as well as ruin your health. "Little blue pills are the answer." No, they are not. In fact, they are a big part of the problem. While you could spend hundreds, and easily thousands, of dollars on drugs like Viagra or Cialis that will work temporarily to give you an erection, they do nothing whatsoever to address the causes of ED.

Not only do these pills not work at all for many men, these drugs can actually destroy your health, leading to blurred vision, increased risk of stroke, blindness, and more. My doctor even warned me that I could be at risk for early heart disease, diabetes, and loss of penile sensitivity. If only more men knew how dangerous those drugs really are.

Even when these drugs do work, it's almost always temporary. After a few months and after causing a bunch of side effects, they stop working.

Now, I have a solution that works just as well — and not temporarily — without a single side effect. And it directly addresses the actual causes of ED.

Now for the third big fat lie, a myth that's created a billion-dollar industry over the past decade. "Testosterone injections will fix your problem." At first, this seems like common sense. After all, testosterone is the male sex hormone and for those who don't stay healthy it does decline with age.

However, what Big Pharma is not telling you is that testosterone injections do not fix ED. They raise your libido, but do nothing to increase blood flow to your penis. In fact, **synthetic testosterone reduces blood flow by creating thicker blood**. The thicker your blood, the worse your circulation becomes, and circulation is absolutely the key to rock-solid erections on demand. So avoid anything that impairs it.

There are some natural alternatives that do not thicken the blood, and you'll learn more about those a little later.

Penis Sensitivity Makes You Both Feel Good

Blood circulation is one piece of the puzzle, but it's

not the only one. There's actually something worse that's happening to your penis. It's something hardly anyone ever talks about and it's at the very root of every case of ED.

Your penis has lost its sensitivity.

You see, your erection is triggered by nerves at the tip that run up and down the shaft. Thanks in part to aggressive masturbation — such as using too tight of a grip, not using proper lubrication, masturbating too frequently, or even prolonged sitting — you can start losing sensitivity in your penis at an alarming rate.

Once these nerves start to die off, every time you masturbate or have sex the skin on your member starts to thicken. This creates the ideal environment for ED to set in. This fact cannot be overstated. The loss of penile sensitivity is probably the number one cause of erectile dysfunction.

The goal of this book and my other courses is to help you restore the sensitivity in your member and revive those dying nerves before they lose all life. Once sensitivity is restored, and your chambers can get more fully engorged leaving you rock hard at the drop of a hat, sexual pleasure explodes. The question is: How do you restore your penile sensitivity and increase the natural flow of blood to your member?

I've seen many men with full-blown ED regain their sexual drive as they watched their withering member reawaken to its younger, harder, fuller self. Or you may be like many men and simply want to have more confidence in your ability to get and keep an erection for as long as it takes to really thrill your wife or lover.

Whatever your particular needs are, I am more than confident that you can get there naturally without modern medicines and all of the side effects they bring with them.

Every ingredient you need is available online or at many health food stores. Imagine the frustration you'll avoid, and the look on your lover's face the first time you sprout the largest and hardest erection you've had in decades.

That's an old age you can look forward to with excitement.

She'll quickly forget all about your past ED problems after the first few times you take her to those exciting new pleasure places.

By staying with these proven formulas, you'll radically increase your penile sensitivity and eradicate your ED for good. However, you'll also discover several simple exercises that you can do by yourself to bring improvement even faster. Trust me, you'll totally enjoy the journey.

Of course, it's not only about you. So you'll be happy to learn about a few positions that have the unique ability of bringing her to orgasm two to five times faster. Believe me when I say, she has no idea what's about to happen to her tonight. Let's just hope you don't mind a little bit of positive gossip.

I've never cheated on my wife, but since I've been practicing these sexual secrets, women have been throwing themselves at me. At first, this really puzzled me, because I've never had that happen before.

I quickly found out that when a man is having frequent sex he releases a very powerful sexual pheromone that attracts women like a magnet. I've had to learn how to resist temptation. Otherwise, my marriage would have been doomed. How you deal with it is your business.

Some men are rather shocked when they once again become hard at the simple thought of having sex with no touching or foreplay required.

And go as long as you desire. Go strong during a few all-nighters. You may not have time for all-nighters all the time, but you'll have the tool and the ammo if you really want to wear her out.

Explode with higher-volume orgasms. The more sensitive your penile shaft is, the more cum you tend to ejaculate.

Lengthen the look and feel of your penis, thanks to those penile chambers receiving the full amount of blood and nitric oxide they need to expand your girth and length to their absolute max.

Switch it up on her and go for all the best positions without fearing the loss of your erection. Most men that have low-level ED stick to only one or two positions to avoid losing their rod. Well, as of today, you can enjoy the sex you want and the sex that your lover truly deserves. Attract more women than ever.

What's really cool is the new-found respect and attention that you'll get from your wife's friends if she starts telling everyone how great her love life is. And she might. You'll become aware when almost every female friend is being extra nice to you and goes out of her way to touch you, hug you, stuff like that.

The secret to all of this is learning to naturally regain full erections without resorting to risky prescription drugs or dangerous surgeries.

Soon, you'll revive your sex life and regain the confidence to perform at a moment's notice —

keeping you healthier and happier.

So, now, you have a very important decision to make, probably one of the most important decisions you'll ever make and one that could dramatically affect your sex life and your future relationships.

If you do nothing, your problems are only going to get worse until you can never get it up again, and the enjoyment and pleasure of sex is nothing but a fading memory. Let's face it, no man wants that. This is your chance to perform sexually on a very high level and keep your partner satisfied — again, without any dangerous medicines and side effects, and without painful surgery.

Because ED doesn't have to be a death sentence. Right now, you stand at the threshold of having the very best sex of your life, assuming you take action. The choice you now face is really no choice at all. I hope you'll walk away from reading this with a renewed hope for what's possible in your sex life.

If you do nothing, if you continue in misery with erectile dysfunction, you risk losing more than just your manhood. Your precious relationship will be an unwilling victim of your ED. Right now, she is slowly pulling away on the inside. Perhaps she's already begun plotting her escape.

Understand, it isn't that she doesn't love you. It's that her body doesn't feel loved by you. A woman's mind is her orgasmic center, and when you can't keep it up long enough to please her and to bring her to the pleasure she's craving, her tender side would rather blame herself than blame you.

Yes, you feel humiliated, embarrassed, less like a man. I've been there so I can relate. However, it's her that feels rejection and misery, and she will have to run to the arms of another man eventually in order to soothe her pain.

Here you will discover a more pleasurable path, one that will put you and your lover on the road to the very best sex of your lives. Sex that's long-lasting, spontaneous, and full of adventure. Sex that combines the confidence she demands in a man, confidence that comes naturally when your member is at your command, with the intimacy that will bind her to you forever.

If you're not in a relationship, if you're single, do you really want to risk making a first impression in the bedroom with a limp sagging member? No man wants this. We crave sexual respect, and to earn that respect you absolutely need to make ED a distant memory.

What you want is to be able to both give and receive all the sexual pleasure in the world. You'll know she craves you and only you, because you can pleasure her like no man ever has. Plus, you'll feel as if someone turned back the clock 10, 20, even 30 years on your sex life. You'll feel just as if you were back in your first girlfriend's bedroom about to score for the very first time before her parents got home from work.

If you can call this a "choice," then the choice is yours, but there's really only one smart choice a man can make.

> Tom from Duluth, Minnesota writes: "Matt, when I first read your book on how to cure ED, I didn't know what to believe. I could tell that you were an honest guy but I thought maybe you didn't have it as bad as I did. I was completely unable to get it up. I couldn't even get it up to masturbate. At 71, I just assumed my time was over. My wife stopped asking for sex over a decade ago. Well, I'm happy to report that I am back in the game, and my dear wife of 44 years could not be happier. She asked that I include you in our Christmas card mailing this year. So, expect a Merry Christmas, and a God Bless from your new friend."

You may find that your new virility creates an occasional awkward erection situation, just like it did when you were a younger man. However, remember that women pick up on your excitement and it actually excites them. Just, act responsibly if you are in a committed relationship!

Will you get too aroused? Your desire will return with a vengeance but you do not run the risk of the extended "blue pill erections" that can literally damage your penis. While the promise of "erections that last for more than four hours" makes for a very good marketing campaign, the reality is that four-hour erections can permanently damage your penile chambers and prevent any future erections.

Many men have lost all hope of ever having an erection again thanks to those dangerous drugs. The good news is you can restore your youthful and natural hardness without them. These natural methods will not cause erections that can damage your manhood.

Will this natural approach make your penis bigger? Simply increasing blood flow to your member will make your penis as big as it can be because your penile chambers will be able to reach maximum blood flow capacity. Rest assured, it will feel thicker and harder to your woman.

The most effective way to prevent penile shrinkage is to have daily erections. Like any muscle, if you don't use it, you lose it. Make sure you use it several times a day if you desire. If you have a heart condition and/or high blood pressure, a natural solution is the best choice you can make.

A healthy diet, supplements, and a little exercise actually serve to protect your heart and lower your blood pressure naturally. So it's completely safe, assuming your doctor has given you the okay to engage in sexual activity.

The ingredients you'll need can be found at grocery stores, local health food stores, or on hundreds of different websites. The key is to know which ingredients to purchase and how to combine them properly.

Your enjoyment of life and the world around you is based on how you feel as a man, and how you feel as a man is based on your ability to perform sexually. Life is short. How many great healthy years do you really have left? I can't promise you that this will add years to your life, but it sure will put the life back into your years.

So, either you continue to miss out on having the

Daniel from New Zealand wrote to say - "I just want to shake your hand one day, mate. I simply cannot believe how well this silly little herbal blend has totally changed my sex life. I'm single, 37, and had ED for over 10 years. Yep, at the ripe old age of 27, my little fella refused to stand to attention. Scared the crap out of me. I did the Viagra thing, and that worked for awhile but then I had a series of kidney problems and I had to stop. I figured I was screwed. No pun intended, until a buddy of mine recommended your book. Now I have women lined up and I'm not joking, I have never had this much sex in my entire life. I know a lot of your customers are older and married, but I'm here to tell you, if you're single this is the greatest thing since the invention of the condom."

-Cheers

intense sexual experiences we are all entitled to as men, or you take dangerous drugs that will make the problem even worse, or you take the best option, the natural option, the only option that makes any sense at all.

Back to our main program, Healthy to 120...

The Main Killer Today

According to the most recent statistics available from the World Health Organization, in 2012 an estimated 56 million people died worldwide. For centuries, worldwide, the most prevalent cause of death was infection and infectious diseases — things like the plague or a cut from rusty barbed wire.

That has now changed big time. Noninfectious diseases were responsible for 68% of all deaths globally in 2012, up from 60% in 2000. <u>The four main noninfectious causes of death are cardiovascular diseases, cancers, diabetes, and chronic lung diseases.</u> Accidental deaths from car accidents, murders, falls, etc. came in at 9% of all deaths.

Low and middle-income countries by far still make up the majority of the world's population. 28 million of the 38 million deaths from noninfectious causes that occurred in 2012 occurred in these countries. However, when broken down proportionately by country, 37% of deaths in low-income countries and 57% in lower middle-income countries were from noninfectious causes. In high-income countries, the number was an astounding 87%.

Measuring how many people die each year and why they died is one of the most important methods — along with gauging how diseases and injuries are affecting people — for assessing the effectiveness of a country's health system.

Cause-of-death statistics help health authorities determine their focus for public health actions. A country where deaths from heart disease and diabetes rapidly rise over a period of a few years, for example, has a strong interest in starting a vigorous program to encourage lifestyles that will help prevent these illnesses.

Keep in mind that noninfectious complications such as cardiovascular diseases, cancers, diabetes, and chronic lung diseases are symptoms mostly brought on by lifestyle choices.

Polyunsaturated Fatty Acids (PUFAs)

Let's have another look at our food supply in recent history, shall we? At the turn of the last century (1900), corn and soybean were fast becoming the largest crops grown in the US. When they started to become by far the cheapest crops we were growing, thanks to government subsidies, the marketing geniuses in the booming agricultural industry conceived a great plan.

And thus began the entire movement toward the use of polyunsaturated fats instead of saturated fats. A few decades later, it peaked with the advent of the lipid hypothesis — the fraudulent claim made by a few bad scientists that convinced everyone that saturated fat and cholesterol were the cause of heart disease and that polyunsaturated fats were better for you.

It's time to set that record straight.

Many decades later...

To this day, saturated fat is still mistakenly thought of as the enemy, while consumption of unsaturated fats, especially PUFA's, are still encouraged by practitioners of mainstream medicine. The result is that we have more heart disease than ever — the "cure" is killing us!

In fact, never before in the history of mankind have we eaten the amount of vegetable oil that we do now. They told us in the '60s that saturated fat was bad for us and that we should use unsaturated fats instead. Several generations have grown up believing that.

Now, everyone's still using unsaturated fats and we're very unhealthy, obesity is an epidemic, and we're dropping dead from all kinds of problems. I'm convinced it's because of these polyunsaturated fatty acids, these bad vegetable oils that we never ate in any quantity before.

Did you know that nuts also contain polyunsaturated fats? I don't eat nuts myself, although they're probably the least harmful form of

PUFA because the most harmful ones are the pure oils that we use for cooking and for bottled salad dressings.

You want to avoid those vegetable oils completely. I would suggest that you use coconut oil or butter instead.

Avoiding PUFAs will also lower your blood pressure and vastly improve your metabolism.

In chemical terms, a PUFA is a fatty acid with more than one (poly) double bond in the carbon chain. They're *un*saturated because they're missing out on something saturated fatty acids have — hydrogen atoms. And that makes the bonds sort of incomplete.

Think of a chain link that's missing a segment or two on each and every link — this isn't very strong or stable. Because of this instability, polyunsaturated fatty acids are very prone to oxidation, which leads the chain to becoming all kinds of messed up and broken. Hence, it causes problems with how your body reacts to the fatty acid.

Ugh, enough chemistry.

But it's really pretty simple. Because of their instability and the negative effects that instability has on the body's systems, these oils are very bad for you — **PUFA is bad.** Saturated is rad!

PUFAs as Omega-3 and Omega-6 Polyunsaturated Fatty Acids

There are two primary types of PUFAs — omega-3 and omega-6 polyunsaturated fatty acids. Don't get caught up in the propaganda around omega-3 being an essential fatty acid. Some early researchers mistook a vitamin B6 deficiency for a fatty acid deficiency. **Omega-3 is NOT an essential fatty acid.** But once they had people hooked on omega-3 products, they kept the profit train rolling.

What is even more dominant in the modern diet are PUFAs in the form of **Omega-6** polyunsaturated fatty acids. Omega-6 fatty acids occur in small quantities in natural foods like seeds, nuts, and legumes, as well as in properly-raised animal products. But very little of our animal products are properly raised these days. What modern science has brought to our dinner tables are animals fed corn and grains and other crap that animals should NOT eat — a steady diet of PUFA-rich food that neither the animals nor people can digest. Instead, it makes people and animals sick.

The biggest problem with omega-6 is that our bodies did not evolve to handle much of it. Our fat cells are comprised of very, very little omega-6 polyunsaturated fatty acids and are instead made up of mostly saturated and monounsaturated fat. So, when we consume the **oils *from* these foods in concentrated form**, instead of eating very small amounts of the actual foods they come from, we wind up with a serious imbalance and the many health problems that result.

Think about it this way. When was the last time you sat down and ate a big bowlful of cotton seeds? You say... **Never!?** Well, thanks to modern technologies in the food processing industry, cottonseed oil is now a very common food. Today, you almost certainly consume it in disgusting quantities. Right along with soybean oil, canola (rapeseed) oil, corn oil, safflower seed oil, sunflower seed oil, and all kinds of these concentrated forms of polyunsaturated fatty acids.

PUFA as a cause of inflammation in the body is slowly becoming recognized. There are other foods that are inflammatory but much less so than PUFAs. Slight inflammation keeps your immune system running smoothly. But when taken to the extreme, inflammation is highly unhealthy. High levels of inflammation have been linked to all sorts of serious conditions, like heart disease, diabetes, and even cancer.

PUFAS cause excessive inflammation in the body because of the presence of **free radicals** formed in the processing of these industrial oils. **Processing** under extremely high pressure and high heat make these industrial oils... not food products.

This renders vegetable oil, canola oil, and other PUFAs rancid. Free radicals, atoms with an unpaired electron floating around, are formed and they basically go nuts. These compounds attack cell membranes and red blood cells. They even cause damage to DNA and RNA strands, leading to cellular mutations in the body's tissues (cancer).

In skin, they cause wrinkles and premature aging. In blood vessels, they lead to the buildup of plaque. In tissues and organs, they can set the stage for tumors to form.

I think you get the picture. Free radicals are bad, bad news, and they're ever-present in industrial PUFA oils that we cook with and eat in processed foods.

In the Good Ol' Days

Take a look at vintage and antique cookbooks with a new set of eyes. I have a couple of cookbooks that date as far back as the late 1800s. You know how everyone is constantly pointing to processed white flour and table sugar as the be-all-end-all reason as to why we're all so fat and unhealthy in our modern age?

That doesn't ring true to me because cookbooks

from the 1800s have white flour and white sugar in their recipes. Lots of it.

People in the 1800s did **NOT** have diabetes and heart disease like we do today. And
they were eating white flour and sugar!

But you know what they weren't consuming?

PUFA OILS

You won't find any vegetable oil, shortening, or any major sources of polyunsaturated fatty acids in any of the recipes from those antique cookbooks. They were still using lard, butter, and other <u>animal fats</u> back then that came from farms, not factories.

Enough said...

Reverse Low Metabolism for Health Improvements

At the risk of repeating myself, low metabolism also has roots in our genetic past. A past that involved feast and famine. Do you think that famines only existed back in cavemen days? Think again. You only need to think about the more recent migrations of millions, people who moved great distances because of the need to find better food sources. Even today, human famine exists in many places in our world.

But people who are well established in first world countries haven't seen famine for several generations. However long it has been, our bodies have not evolved away from the desire and need for survival during famine. Instinctive survival is a major factor when it comes to a low and slow metabolism.

When your body reacts to slow your metabolism, it's all about one thing: **survival!** It's not about your body trying to conspire against you to ruin your life. It's your body making a wise decision to sacrifice long-term health for short-term survival when its being told to do so because of food and nutrient scarcity. The slowing of the metabolism allows your body to go LONGER on less food. The body also tends to hold on to fat as a protective mechanism.

This certainly seems ridiculous in light of the obese society we live in today. **With our sedate lifestyle, the time when we need to convert fat back into energy never comes.** Long gone are the famines when fat was needed for our very survival.

We've already taken a look at high blood pressure, its related diseases, and the awful side effects that high blood pressure medicines bring on. You also now know that what has been published as the "medical standard" for blood pressure is too low for most people.

However, high blood pressure can be a symptom of a low metabolism. I encourage you to find alternatives to high blood pressure medication, and overcoming low metabolism is one very good alternative.

High blood pressure can mean there are some problems with your body's metabolism that might cause other health issues like diabetes if you don't address them. By addressing those problems, you're going to prevent a lot of other problems and make your body work better all around.

These issues are very, very basic to metabolism and very, very important. So, by fixing blood pressure — the way we're going to be talking about it — all of these other potential problems (things like the chances of getting a heart attack or a stroke, and diminished mental acuity) are going to be much, less of a concern for much longer.

Restoring low minerals levels to healthy levels helps most people. These include potassium, calcium, magnesium, and sodium. Insufficient levels of those minerals in your body can cause high blood pressure. Possibly half of the people with high blood pressure can fix it just by restoring those minerals.

Another culprit that causes high blood pressure and ultimately low metabolism is stress in your body. We've already covered this extensively, but you might want to review it.

If your blood pressure is at an acceptable level and you're getting the correct exercise, you want to consider these other factors that can lead to slow metabolism (these include dramatically lowering or completely removing PUFAs from your diet):

❖ **Nutrition deficiencies**: Fat soluble vitamin deficiencies have become common as a result of the popularity of low-fat diets, as well as some other common nutrient deficiencies.

❖ **Malnourished liver**: Often caused by not enough high-quality animal protein. Common in those with a history of veganism or low protein vegetarian diet.

❖ **Poor digestion**: Weak digestion down-regulates or reduces the appetite. This is often due to bloating or constipation that are often the cause of not being able to take in enough. Think of inflammation-related physiological stress here.

❖ **Hormonal imbalance**: Low progesterone levels or estrogen dominance can slow the metabolism by interfering with the body's ability to convert thyroid hormone.

❖ **Poor liver detoxification**: Leaves excess toxins in the diet. An unhealthy lifestyle along with poor liver detoxification are a real burden on the metabolism.

❖ **Stress**: The stress hormone cortisol blocks thyroid hormone conversion, which protectively slows metabolism over time.

❖ **Inflammation**: Food sensitivities, food allergies, polyunsaturated fats (PUFAs) are common causes of inflammation.

❖ **Over-exercising**: Too much exercise, especially when the diet is poor, is a sure way to send your body running for safety by slowing the metabolism.

Be patient with your body. You didn't get a slow metabolism overnight and recovery won't happen in a day, a week, a month, six months, or even a year in some cases! Understand that your body is doing the best it can to re-balance.

The Cox-Prostaglandins-Estrogen-Fibrosis Link

Okay, we need to get a little technical here again...

The fact that **vitamin E** can be an estrogen opponent, energy promoter, and anti-inflammatory probably runs counter to what you have previously read in medical publications if you have the same nerdy hobby of reading health journals that I have.

What used to totally shock me is how easily the tight connection between political ambition and corporate greed spills over into respected medical publications. Today, I agree with what Dr. Ray Peat has to say about this connection in his article "Vitamin E: Estrogen antagonist, energy promoter, and anti-inflammatory:"

> *"Vitamin E, like progesterone and aspirin, acts within the cellular regulatory systems, to prevent inflammation and inappropriate excitation. Since uncontrolled excitation causes destructive oxidations, these substances prevent those forms of oxidation.*
>
> *Molecules that can easily be oxidized and reduced can function as antioxidants, and vitamin E does function as that kind of antioxidant in many chemical environments. But it is highly misleading to consider that as the explanation for its many beneficial biological effects. That kind of reasoning contributed to the use of the antioxidant carcinogens BHT and BHA as food additives and 'antiaging 'supplements, and many other chemicals are being promoted on the basis of their abstract antioxidant function.*
>
> *Becoming aware of the real value of vitamin E will have far reaching implications in nutrition and medicine.*

In determining criminal or civil legal responsibility, the concept 'should have known' is recognized and used. In science, which is all about knowing, there is certainly a responsibility to be informed when the subject involves the life and health of millions of people. The science establishment of government and industry should be held responsible for the information it hides, destroys, or ignores for its own benefit. The US government has an agency for prosecuting research fraud, but the concept is applied so narrowly as to be meaningless, when deception has become the rule. And since it controls the court system, government agencies and their functionaries won't be prosecuted, even when their crimes become well known.

Vitamin E was advocated as an effective treatment for heart disease by Dr. Evan Shute of London, Ontario more than 50 years ago. His pioneering claims, which were unacceptable to the medical community at large, have been confirmed by recent findings from epidemiologic studies and clinical trials."

During the 1930s and 1940s, Dr. Shute (followed soon by his sons, Wilfred and Evan) was actively studying the benefits and effects of vitamin E. Both estrogen and vitamin E were being widely studied at the same time. Vitamin E was found to improve fertility of both male and female animals and to prevent miscarriages, so it was called the "anti-sterility vitamin."

Animal research in the 1930s was also showing that estrogen had many toxic effects, including causing infertility, stillbirth, connective tissue abnormalities, and excessive blood clotting.

As studies progressed, Dr. Shute and his sons came to conclude that vitamin E could be used to counter the effects of estrogen. This did not please the estrogen industry.

Other researchers, who knew that progesterone protected against the toxic effects of estrogen, described vitamin E as the "progesterone-sparing agent", since so many of its anti-estrogen effects resembled those of progesterone.

The Shute brothers began using vitamin E to treat circulatory diseases in general rather than just in pregnant women. Blood clots, phlebitis, hypertension, heart disease, and diabetes all responded well to treatment with large doses of vitamin E.

What transpired from the 1930s into the 1980s was a quagmire of bad science, much of it perpetuated by the same doctors and scientists that once convinced Americans that smoking was good for them. At that time, smoking was even supported by the American Medical Association (AMA). This is a classic representation of bad medicine aiding industrial greed.

Coming out of all this misinformation was that estrogen was labeled "the female hormone." Natural hormones, including estrogen and progesterone, it was claimed, without any research, were inactive when taken orally. Physician-shills were created to make wonderful claims about the effects of estrogen.

The vitamin status of the tocopherols (a family of vitamin E compounds) was denied as recently as the 1970s (and maybe later). University dietetics professors were stating flatly that "no one needs vitamin E."

A 1981 article published in the journal of the AMA reviewed the "toxic" effects of vitamin E. Very importantly, the author claimed that analysis of the cited articles led to the conclusion that whenever vitamin E changed something, the change was harmful. This was major fraud because the originally cited publication had described the effects as beneficial.

In the 1940s, the official definition of vitamin E's activity was changed. Instead of noting its effectiveness in preventing the death of embryos, or the degeneration of the testicles, brain, or muscles, it was redefined as an antioxidant, preventing the oxidation of unsaturated oils.

During this time, there was a lot more going on in the estrogen and PUFA industries. By the late 1940s and early 1950s, estrogens of various sorts had been manufactured from hydrocarbons. These were recommended to prevent miscarriages, because "estrogen is the female hormone."

About the same time, the meat industry soon found polyunsaturated oils were valuable in animal feed because these suppressed metabolism and made it cheaper to fatten the animals. And these unsaturated oils were next marketed as "heart protective" foods for humans with the selling point that they suppress the thyroid and destroy vitamin E.

In reality, unsaturated oils actually contribute to both heart disease and cancer. This move to polyunsaturated food sources was very beneficial to industry but extremely unhealthy for humans.

The influence of the food oil industry kept researchers away from the idea that these oils were not safe for food use and instead tended to support the idea that vitamin E is just an antioxidant, and that seed oils were the best way to get vitamin E into the diet.

Dr. Ray Peat concludes:

> 'The enzymes that, if we didn't eat PUFA,
> would be regulating the Mead series... [fatty
> acid strongly inhibited by PUFA seed oils]
> being activated in response to stress, would
> be producing antistress substances, which
> would limit the stress reaction. But as we
> become increasingly saturated with the anti-
> vitamin E fats, these enzymes, instead of
> stopping inflammation, promote it and cause
> tissue injury. The remaining stress limiting
> factors, such as progesterone, by correcting
> the distortions caused by stress, tend to
> eliminate the conditions which activated the
> enzymes — in a very indirect form of
> inhibition.
>
> Many of the events involved in inflammation
> are increased by estrogen, and decreased by
> vitamin E. Estrogen causes capillaries to
> become leaky; vitamin E does the opposite.
> Estrogen increases platelet aggregation, and
> decreases a factor that inhibits platelet
> aggregation; vitamin E does the opposite.
>
> Excess clotting is known to be caused by too
> much estrogen, and also by a vitamin E
> deficiency.
>
> Clotting leads to fibrosis, and there is clear
> evidence that vitamin E prevents and cures

fibrotic diseases, but this still isn't generally accepted by the powerful medical institutions. Estrogen and polyunsaturated fats increase fibrosis.

Estrogen often increases intracellular calcium and protein kinase C, vitamin E has generally opposite effects.

The polyunsaturated fatty acids and their derivatives, the prostaglandins, act as effectors, or amplifiers, of estrogen's actions.

If vitamin E is acting as a protectant against the polyunsaturated fatty acids, that in itself would account for at least some of its antiestrogenic effects."

Slow or Stop Oxidative Phosphorylation

Although oxidative phosphorylation is a vital part of metabolism, it produces reactive oxygen species such as superoxide and **hydrogen peroxide.** Oxygen radicals tend to be very reactive and can damage many of the most important macromolecules in the body. The superoxide radical is only moderately reactive. However, it is soon converted to hydrogen peroxide, which soon becomes hypochlorite. **This is bleach! It readily kills almost any microorganism.**

This entire proliferation of free radicals is damaging

to cells and contributes to disease and possibly aging. The enzymes carrying out this metabolic pathway are also the target of many drugs and poisons that inhibit their activities.

Hydrogen peroxide, one of those free radicals, is damaging to the body. If Fe++ (iron) or another heavy metal is present, the hydrogen peroxide is readily converted to the hydroxyl radical. The hydroxyl radical is very reactive and damages most macromolecules, including DNA, proteins, and lipids.

Bad stuff all the way around.

Determining the Rate of Oxidative Phosphorylation

The most important factor in determining the rate of oxidative phosphorylation is the level of adenosine triphosphate (ATP). It is often referred to as the "molecular unit of currency."

The rate of oxygen consumption by mitochondria (known as the powerhouses of the cell) increases markedly when ATP is added. These act like a digestive system that takes in nutrients, breaks them down, and creates energy-rich molecules for the cell.

The mitochondrial oxidative phosphorylation (OxPhos) system plays a key role in energy production, the generation of free radicals, and apoptosis. A lack of cellular energy, excessive radical production, and programmed cell death are found alone or in combination in most human diseases, including neurodegenerative diseases, stroke, cardiovascular disorders, ischemia/reperfusion, and cancers.

What this means is that the adjustment of energy production to physiological demand is essential to the proper functioning of all higher organisms.

Regulation of oxidative phosphorylation is controlled by the energy needs of our cells.

When the amount of ATP available is in excess of the body's requirements, the liver uses the excess ATP and excess glucose to produce molecules called glycogen (a polymeric form of glucose) that is stored in the liver and skeletal muscle cells.

Here is a good explanation from an article called "Food Energy and ATP" on Boundless.com:

> *'When blood sugar drops, the liver releases glucose from its stores of glycogen. Skeletal muscle converts glycogen to glucose during intense exercise. The process of converting glucose and excess ATP to glycogen and the storage of excess energy is an evolutionarily-important step in helping animals deal with mobility, food shortages, and famine."*

The problem is that in today's society most of us never need this reserve energy. It's a significant contributor to obesity and causes complications for those with diabetes.

In a recent study (the report is on the American Diabetes Association's website) researchers induced mice to:

> "...overexpress protein targeting to glycogen (PTG) in the liver (PTG(OE)), which results in an increase in liver glycogen. When fed a high-fat diet (HFD), these animals reduced their food intake. The resulting effect was a lower body weight, decreased fat mass, and reduced leptin levels. Furthermore, PTG overexpression reversed the glucose intolerance and hyperinsulinemia caused by the HFD and protected against HFD-induced hepatic steatosis."

The report goes on:

"Additionally, after an overnight fast, PTG(OE) animals showed high liver glycogen content, lower liver triacylglycerol content, and lower serum concentrations of fatty acids and β-hydroxybutyrate compared to control mice, regardless whether they received a HFD or a standard diet (SD).

In conclusion, liver glycogen accumulation caused a reduced food intake, protected against the harmful effects of a high fat diet, and diminished the metabolic impact of fasting.

Therefore, we propose that liver glycogen content be considered a potential target for the pharmacological manipulation of diabetes and obesity."

While I certainly don't come to the same conclusion that this proves a need for pharmacological manipulation of diabetes and obesity, it does demonstrate the importance of monitoring your good sugar intake and increasing your intake of good carbs and some proteins, while supplementing your diet with vitamin E.

Diabetes Treatments Are NOT Healthy

Type 2 diabetes is directly caused by lifestyle. Type 2 diabetics do NOT need drugs. In fact, taking drugs for type 2 diabetes can be far worse than the disease itself!

Drugs are widely prescribed for type 2 diabetics to help lower blood sugar levels, but a new meta-analysis of 13 randomized controlled trials involving more than 33,000 people showed that this treatment is not only ineffective, it's dangerous as well. Treatment with glucose-lowering drugs actually showed the potential of increasing your risk of death from heart-related disease and all other causes.

That study was published in *BMJ* in 2011 and concluded:

> *"The overall results of this meta-analysis do not show a benefit of intensive glucose lowering treatment on all cause mortality or cardiovascular death. A 19% increase in all cause mortality and a 43% increase in cardiovascular mortality cannot be excluded."*

Note: "all cause" mortality is a grouping of miscellaneous deaths.

Furthermore, if diabetes medicines are of particular interest to you, you should read the details of the Action to Control Cardiovascular Risk in Diabetes (ACCORD) study. This was a large (more than 10,000 type 2 diabetics) government-funded study designed to evaluate the effectiveness of various medication regimens for reducing heart attacks, strokes, and death from heart disease in patients with type 2 diabetes.

One part of the study was specifically set up to test the widely-held assumption that more aggressive lowering of blood sugar would provide greater protection against heart disease.

However, in February 2008, that part of the

ACCORD study was abruptly shut down because it found that just the opposite was true. Study participants who were on the most intensive drug regimens aimed at driving down blood sugar had a much higher cardiovascular death rate.

This is highly disturbing, but certainly not news, considering researchers have known about the fatal complications of diabetes medications since 1969, when results of the University Group Diabetes Program were made public.

Just like ACCORD, this study had to be stopped two years early when **participants who were taking diabetes medications had a 250%-300% higher death rate than those taking the placebo.**

Here are some known facts about specific diabetes medications:

❖ **Phenformin/metformin (Glucophage):** One of the two drugs used in the 1969 study, DBI (phenformin), was shown to be so deadly that it was taken off the market. Still, this drug's close companion, metformin (glucophage) is the most popular diabetes medication used today and was the most frequently-used drug in the ACCORD study.

❖ **Sulfonylureas:** The other drug used in the 1969 study, Orinase (tolbutamide), was ultimately labeled with a warning stating that it dramatically increases the risk of death from heart attack. Orinase belongs to a class of drugs known as sulfonylureas, which includes dozens of popular medications that are still in use today, and the same warning has appeared on all sulfonylureas since 1984.

❖ **Thiazolinediones (glitazones):** Another class of diabetes medications (the second most widely-used type of drugs of the ACCORD study participants) is one that government experts estimate may have caused as many as 100,000 heart attacks since coming onto the market in 1999 (the most notorious of which is Avandia).

IMPORTANT NOTE: If you are currently taking an oral hypoglycemic drug, don't stop taking it cold turkey. You must work with your doctor to gradually discontinue the medication.

Diabetes Medicines Don't Help Neuropathy

Neuropathy (the term used to describe a problem with the nerves, usually the peripheral nerves) is a well-known symptom of diabetes. High blood sugar can cause diabetic neuropathy, which damages the nerves that send signals from your hands and feet.

Diabetic neuropathy can cause numbness or tingling in your fingers, toes, hands, and feet. Another symptom is a burning sensation, or a sharp or aching pain (diabetic nerve pain). The pain may be mild at first, but it can get worse over time and spread up your legs or arms. Walking can be painful and even the softest touch can feel unbearable. Eventually, doctors may recommend amputations of extremities of your body. Is this the" cure" you're looking for?

There are ways that you can naturally prevent further nerve damage and relieve your pain. Control your blood sugar so the damage doesn't progress. Sugar itself is not the problem. The problem is the control of blood sugar. Stay active and eat a healthy diet to decrease your blood sugar to a healthier range. Avoid the pharmaceuticals that cause far more damage and don't cure diabetes.

If you do decide to continue with medicines to relieve neuropathy pain, here is what you can expect doctors to suggest (progressively):

Over-the-counter pain relievers such as aspirin, Tylenol, or ibuprofen, which are available without a prescription but can cause side effects.

Antidepressants are intended to treat depression. However, they can be prescribed for diabetic nerve pain because they interfere with chemicals in your brain that cause you to feel pain. A doctor may recommend tricyclic antidepressants such as amitriptyline (Elavil), imipramine (Tofranil), and desipramine (Norpramin). These can cause unpleasant side effects like dry mouth, fatigue, and sweating. Your doctor may not recommend tricyclic antidepressants if you have a history of heart problems.

Serotonin and norepinephrine reuptake inhibitors such as venlafaxine (Effexor) and duloxetine (Cymbalta) are alternatives to tricyclics and tend to have fewer side effects.

Opioid pain medicines are very strong drugs such as oxycodone, and the opioid-like medicine tramadol (Conzip, Ultram) which can treat much stronger pain. But these are a last resort for pain relief. You might use these medications if other treatments aren't working. However, these drugs are not meant for long-term relief because of side effects and the potential for addiction. Use extreme caution when taking opioid medicines.

Lidocaine patches deliver local anesthetic through a patch placed on the skin and can also cause minor skin irritation.

Anti-seizure drugs meant to prevent epileptic seizures can also be used to treat nerve pain. These drugs include pregabalin, gabapentin, phenytoin, and carbamazepine. Pregabalin can also improve your sleep. Side effects include drowsiness, swelling, and dizziness.

Do you really want to do this? You could take fistfuls of drugs for symptoms but wouldn't you rather cure your diabetes altogether?

Type 2 Diabetes Can be Cured

Never let anyone (not even a doctor, and especially not a pharma rep) tell you that type 2 diabetes has no cure. It's true that it has no pharmaceutical cure, but the much better alternative is simply adopting a naturally healthy lifestyle.

Type 2 diabetes is not terminal. You don't have to live with it until it or the medicines kill you! Nearly 100% of type 2 diabetics can be successfully cured. That means eliminating both the symptoms of diabetes and the high risk of developing health complications. These same changes also drastically reduce your risk of developing the disease in the first place.

Instead of curing diabetes by reversing the inflammation that causes diabetes, the drug companies are selling diabetics fistfuls of pills every day... **And, even worse, the average diabetic's life expectancy is ten years shorter...**

Plus, diabetics face other diseases... weight gain, high blood pressure, prostate problems, and erectile dysfunction...

It's not blood sugar that's the problem, and it's

not too much salt. It's the inflammation. Fix the inflammation and you fix the diabetes. And you DON'T need their fistfuls of pills...

So, are you ready to get rid of your diabetes?

❖ Begin by significantly limiting or eliminating bad sugar (artificial sweeteners) and grains from your diet. Go for natural sugar. A good one is fructose. It's found in fruits and widely used as a sweetener in other foods and beverages.

❖ Take a close look at your diet and especially look for hidden sources of artificial sweeteners.

Following my nutrition plan will help you do this without much fuss. It's important to realize that nearly all type 2 diabetics need to swap out their grains for other foods such as healthy sources of protein.

❖ Staying active is essential. Without it, you're highly unlikely to get this devastating disease under control. It is clearly one of the most powerful ways to lower your insulin and leptin resistance. Make sure to incorporate high-intensity Peak Fitness exercises. This type of exercise boosts fat loss, promotes muscle building, and helps your body produce human growth hormone (HGH) naturally.

❖ Eat saturated fats, such as grass-fed organic meat, dairy products, and coconut oil. Saturated fats provide a concentrated source of energy along with the building blocks for cell membranes and a variety of hormones and hormone-like substances. When you eat healthy fats as part of your meal, they slow down absorption so that you go longer without feeling hungry again. In addition, they act as carriers for the important fat-soluble vitamins A, D, E, and K.

Enough bad news, the better news is The Main Secret to Living to 120! (Read on...)

The Main Secrets to Being Healthy to 120

Keeping in mind that the subtitle of this book is "Surviving and Thriving Despite Modern Medicine," and that it has now been well established that the primary objective of pharmaceutical companies is making money at any expense including human life, let's take a closer look at a more objective study of what these **for profit businesses** are really up to.

After all, these "miracle" drugs and treatments are the cornerstone of modern medicine. If you've read this far, you've been forewarned that you almost certainly want to avoid them if you want to live a long and healthy life...

Big Pharma Chemicals Subjected To Real Study

The reason that I keep picking on statins is that they are so widely prescribed. Statin drugs cause type 2 diabetes. And these show a relationship to ALS-like symptoms. I don't think statins should ever be taken. <u>These drugs are all risk without any meaningful reward.</u>

Statins are pushed, promoted, and peddled by Big Pharma. Busy doctors are unable to discern the truth, so they prescribe what Big Pharma tells them is best. That leaves it up to us to try to figure it all out.

I need to tell you some very earth-shattering and disturbing evidence about why you should stop taking statins, or at least talk to your doctor about other options. I'd really like for you to show this to your doctor.

First of all, I believe the giant studies that involve numbers like 100,000 people are usually bogus. Why?

Well, it's simple. The result that they're trying to prove has such a small effect **they need to have 100,000 study subjects to show any effect at all.** That's why this study I'm about to tell you about is so critical: It's not one of those bogus studies, it's a **REAL STUDY.** You can find it here: https://www.ncbi.nlm.nih.gov/pmc/articles/PMC4 285455/.

The researchers divided about 1,000 participants (two-thirds men and one-third women) into groups, and the groups were given various doses of either statins or placebo. This was a double blind study, meaning neither the researchers nor the men and women in the study knew if they were getting a real statin or the placebo. And a variety of statins were used, not just one, meaning results could not be attributed to one specific brand.

What they found will disturb you, especially if you've been taking statins.

The statins made people feel very tired and rundown. They interfered with their lives and their lifestyles. While the effects were worse for women than for men, they were bad for both. **Moreover, it wasn't just a few people** who suffered complications and side effects. **It was a LOT of people.**

20%-25% of men noticed more fatigue, tiredness, and difficulty moving around. Even more women, up to 40%, noticed this. And remember, these were **LOW** doses of statins, about one-quarter to one-half of what Big Pharma companies recommend for "intense" use.

According to the researchers:

> *"...unfavorable statin effects on energy and exertional fatigue... were seen in a generally healthy sample given modest statin doses."*

And:

> *"...both simvastatin and pravastatin contributed to the significant adverse effect of statins on energy and fatigue with exertion."*

That's very bad, because thousands of people have

to take the statins for them to have a positive effect on even just one or two people. **The number of people "needed to treat" is around a thousand just to save ONE life.**

Meanwhile all the other 999 are suffering various health problems and lifestyle issues.

But of course it gets worse...

Now, we get into real skullduggery and villainy. That's not to say that the Big Pharma companies outright misled, lied, and cheated, because I have no way to prove it.

I do know that they use statistical methods to try to put their best foot forward. **And most doctors don't have the time to really sit down and analyze all the studies.**

But that's what people like me do. And what I find rarely matches what doctors are being told.

For example, you may have heard of ALS (amyotrophic lateral sclerosis) or Lou Gehrig's disease. Well, it turns out there is a strong link between statins and something that resembles ALS.

I mentioned skullduggery... here's why:

The Big Pharma companies have helped to **PREVENT** research on the tie between statins and this ALS-like disease. One way they've done this is through nomenclature. They've done such a good job of that — if you look up ALS and statins, you don't find much. They keep that out of the search engines because the ALS-like symptoms are also called neuromuscular degeneration in the nomenclature, and most people aren't going to think of "neuromuscular degeneration" when they look up their symptoms online. And it gets more confusing because a definitive diagnosis of ALS is rather difficult to nail down to begin with.

Many people have ALS-like symptoms.

You might as well say they have ALS, but some doctors and diagnosticians will argue that point.

What is clear is that there is a vast underreporting of ALS-like symptoms among statin users. This means that if you take statins you are much more likely to get ALS or something like ALS.

But ALS or ALS lookalikes are not listed in the side effects for statins, so no one realizes it. Pity the poor scientists who are working on this, because there is no funding on anything else for researching this connection.

There is even active resistance on the part of the various medical journals that get most of their financial support from Big Pharma companies. I'm not saying the journals are deliberately squashing the research. But most people are reluctant to say something that could damage their bottom line. The people running these journals walk that line between honest reporting and needing to keep their printing presses running.

Researchers who published a study under the title "Statins, neuromuscular degenerative disease and an amyotrophic lateral sclerosis-like syndrome: an analysis of individual case safety reports from vigibase" issued what almost amounts to an apology in their conclusion:

> *"We emphasise the rarity of this possible association, and also the need for further study to establish whether a causal relationship exists.*
>
> *We do advocate that trial discontinuation of a statin should be considered in patients with serious neuromuscular disease such as the ALS-like syndrome, given the poor prognosis and a possibility that progression of the disease may be halted or even reversed."*

But how rare is neuromuscular degeneration and/or ALS-like symptoms among statin users, really? I think it's much, much more common than these researchers indicated. First of all, it's staggeringly common for statin users to experience muscle aches and pains. Sometimes they develop permanent disability and pain in their muscles.

It's extraordinarily common.

I've known a number of people who have had this happen to them. And it didn't get better when they stopped taking statins either.

Here's a study that contains some shocking numbers: "Mild to Moderate Muscular Symptoms with High-Dosage Statin Therapy in Hyperlipidemic Patients – The PRIMO Study" — even if they didn't get ALS or an ALS-like syndrome, a lot of people experienced very significant muscle damage.

> *"Overall, muscular symptoms were reported by 832 patients (10.5%), with a median time of onset of 1 month following initiation of statin therapy.*
>
> *Muscular pain prevented even moderate exertion during everyday activities in 315 patients (38%), while 31 (4%) were confined to bed or unable to work."*

I've said again and again that there is simply no excuse for prescribing statins. This is one of the worst Big Pharma chemicals that's ever been prescribed. And the extent to which they're pulling the wool over our eyes and our doctors 'eyes is simply astounding.

I hope that you will look at the studies together with your doctor and discuss some alternatives. If you know someone on statins, you might want to share these studies with them.

Not surprisingly, I could show you many more studies that debunk what pharmaceutical companies are spoon-feeding the medical community and ultimately you, me, and rest of the public at large. But I think I've shown you a clear enough picture to persuade you to always question (in deep detail) any medications and treatments prescribed for symptoms for which intestinal inflammation is the root cause and that can therefore be fully cured through diet, exercise, and a few lifestyle changes.

Now, let's look at what you can do to ensure a long healthy life while remaining sexually robust...

Metabolism for Long Life

Increasing your rate of metabolism gives you more energy, and that helps you lose weight and improves your ability to stay more active or exercise more. Having a slow metabolism is almost always a function of what you eat. When you take this down another step to the root cause, you'll almost certainly find that slow metabolism, being overweight, and difficulty staying active are all rooted in intestinal inflammation.

Take another look at what you've already learned about overcoming a slow metabolism. The problems are nutritional deficiencies, including deficiencies in fat-soluble vitamins due to low-fat diets, a malnourished liver due to insufficient consumption of high quality animal protein, and the ever-devastating diet that's high in PUFAs.

Your heart rate, as a measure of metabolism, indicates that longer-living people have a slower heart rate. So maybe there is something to the adage that your heart has a limited number of beats in your lifetime. We all know that exercise increases your heart rate, so it would follow that lower-intensity exercise leads to a longer life. Science will never outsmart evolution.

What you want is regular **anaerobic** exercise that elevates your heart rate for short periods of time. **Anaerobic exercise is defined as short-duration, high-intensity exercise** lasting anywhere from mere seconds up to around two minutes. After two minutes, the body's **aerobic** system kicks in.

Examples of anaerobic exercise are ones that use fast-twitch muscle fibers. Good examples are jumping and sprinting. By using and developing those muscle fibers, we enhance that musculature.

This is not endurance exercise. Building up your heart muscle through short burst of activity enables it to pump more blood (thus a slower heart beat) when it's at rest.

I'm not sure about the limited number of heart beats per life thing, but relatively slow at-rest heart beat indicates a healthy metabolism.

Other causes of an out-of-balance metabolism include:

❖ Poor digestion

❖ Stress

❖ Hormonal imbalance

❖ Poor liver detoxification

❖ Over-exercising

Mitochondrial Uncoupling – Fight Aging

Mitochondria are the power plants of your cells. They turn food into ATP, used as fuel by the cell. In recent years, the research community has turned some attention to the process of mitochondrial uncoupling. This is when the processing of food is uncoupled from the generation of ATP, which results in less ATP and more energy in the form of heat – part of the temperature regulation system in mammals. It is also important in calorie restriction and therefore important to longevity and aging.

Get this right and you'll again have the metabolism of a teenager.

Dieting (low fat or no fat) is NOT the answer to losing weight and is certainly not the answer to boosting your metabolism. Starving your body of good fats slows your metabolism and robs you of energy. A slow metabolism is a physiological response to starvation — your body has gone into survival mode. All of your physiological functions slow down and this can literally bring your sex response to a stop. After all, sex isn't critical to your survival.

DNP (2,4-dinitrophenol) raises metabolism and was introduced in the 1930s as a drug to treat obesity. What does DNP do? It causes mitochondrial uncoupling, i.e. it increases proton leak and, as a result, energy production becomes less efficient. Patients treated with DNP therefore waste more energy and their metabolic rate increases. This increase in energy output while energy intake remains constant means that people will start losing weight.

But it doesn't stop with weight loss. With a higher metabolism you can fend off common medical conditions like heart disease, high blood pressure, type 2 diabetes, and others, including erectile dysfunction.

In the DNP studies of the 1930s, no increase in heart rate was noted. Patients receiving daily doses of 3 to 5 mg/kg experienced a 40% increase in metabolic rate that was maintained for at least ten weeks. After those ten weeks, a mean weight loss of seventeen pounds was observed. So, there was no need for dieting.

With that said, DNP can be dangerous. It can cause eye problems or even blindness and is NOT recommended.

The same effects from DNP can be accomplished with aspirin and caffeine and other natural compounds that have been proven safe over decades or centuries.

And there is much more that you can do for a long enjoyable life...

Just to be crystal clear: I'm not talking about tottering around a nursing home at 90 years old. I'm talking about being 100 or 110, living on your own, eating all the foods you love, socializing with the people you love, having great sex every day, and living a life that would be envied by a 20-year-old.

Reduce Health Stress for a Longer Healthy Life

Good health requires minimizing stress hormones in the body.

That doesn't mean you're minimizing stress in your life. Sometimes stress in your life actually contributes to long life.

But it does mean minimizing the stress hormones in your body, including cortisol, estrogen, serotonin, and adrenaline.

The hormones you need to increase are the ones that are high-energy, that build lean muscle mass, and that build bone mass, such as progesterone, dopamine, and testosterone.

Now, how do you do that...?

Drugs — OR — Supplements and Herbs

The use of herbal supplements has a long history dating back thousands of years. Today, Western cultures tend to consume foods that are high in calories, but lack nutrients that are vital for good health (processed foods). Herbs and other supplements can enhance our poor Western diets, but you should first **rely on a healthy carbohydrate diet and eliminate PUFAs** before turning to supplements to make up for missing nutrients.

Herbal supplements are sold in many different forms — powders, dried leaves for teas, as capsules or tablets, or in solution. Almost 20% of Americans currently take some type of herbal or non-herbal supplement.

When you are ready to lower your high blood pressure and take control of diabetes to bring your body and sex life back from the abyss that modern diets have brought us to, you need to begin at the molecular level. **Herbs, micronutrients, and probiotics do exactly that: work at the cellular level to nourish your body with what is needed to regain your health.**

You'll actually need more natural sugar at some point. Make sure you are monitoring your blood sugar levels and working with your doctor.

You can then add in magnesium... this is ULTRA important as diabetics are always dangerously low in magnesium (and it isn't an instant fix either).

WARNING:
Listen to your body. Some of these are VERY potent. Some will disagree with you unless you are already eating well. And some may even be harmful for you. Be SURE to speak to your DOCTOR before taking ANY of these. Speak to your pharmacist too.

Supplements and Herbs
Here is a partial list of supplements and herbs that you want to consider adding to your diet. Stay tuned because this list is frequently updated as more research and information become available.

❖ **Niacinamide** (vitamin supplement): lowers blood

sugar and kick-starts the cells into burning sugar!

❖ **Thiamine** (vitamin supplement): lowers ammonia levels in the brain and body.

❖ **Taurine** (supplement): activates sugar burning. May cause a bit of heartburn as it stimulates production of digestive enzymes from the gallbladder.

❖ **Lysine** (supplement): combats gut inflammation.

❖ **B6 P5P form** (vitamin supplement): extremely powerful in lowering prolactin and raising dopamine.

❖ **Biotin** (vitamin supplement): potent for lowering blood sugar.

❖ **Collagen** (supplement): can be used as is. Gelatin can be substituted but requires some additional processing.

❖ **Branched chain amino acids (BCAA)** (supplement): lowers serotonin levels in the brain.

❖ **L-phenylalanine or tyrosine** (supplement): works synergistically with branched chain amino acids.

❖ **Natural sugar** (supplement): strange but true, it really helps lower fatty acids and cortisol, and will help prevent low blood sugar. You may need a LOT more sugar for a time.

❖ **Theanine** (supplement): helps to calm you down, reduces cortisol, and also reduces allergies.

❖ **DHEA** (hormone supplement): helpful in lowering cortisol levels.

❖ **Methylene blue** (supplement): reduces nitric oxide, raises metabolism, improves sugar burning, lowers estrogen, and raises testosterone.

❖ **Magnesium** (supplement): may make your butt sore. It can be tricky getting enough but it is CRITICAL.

❖ **Ceylon cinnamon** (optional supplement): lowers blood sugar and lowers ammonia levels in the brain.

❖ **Aspirin:** CAUTION, start with a tiny sliver of aspirin and follow the aspirin protocol (move up slowly to make sure you tolerate it). Aspirin can

CURE diabetics and is beneficial in many other ways.

❖ **Progesterone:** counteracts high estrogen.

❖ **Pregnenolone:** HUGELY helpful. It VASTLY calms you, lowers stress hormones like nothing else, and restores normal metabolism.

Probiotics

I keep ALL my probiotics in the refrigerator. They last longer that way.

❖ **Saccharomyces boulardii:** great remedy for runny stool and getting rid of dangerous infections such as *C. difficile* in the bowel. It is very safe for almost everyone (except very severely immune-compromised people).

❖ **Bifido:** an outstanding probiotic that makes a dramatic difference in only a few days. I've found you don't need to keep taking it. I take it with a bit of psyllium fiber before bedtime a few nights in a row. It's expensive though.

❖ **Psyllium:** detoxes the liver. Use two tablespoons every day in the beginning. Use an unrefined version, take with plenty of water. This binds liver bile and removes toxins through the bowel.

Add your Bifido to it. Stop taking it after you are regular. Long term use may be cancer-causing.

❖ **Phages:** for treating pathogenic bacterial infections and removing bad bacteria from the small intestine.

Minerals and Vitamins

Minerals and vitamins contain micronutrients each of which benefits your body in unique ways. For example, Vitamin K Mk type 4 has many health benefits beyond raising T-levels. It aids in mineral absorption and helps your metabolism. It has been shown to reduce the risks of cardiovascular disease and pneumonia. **Taking vitamin K along with vitamins A and D has a synergistic effect: It increases the effectiveness of vitamins A and D.**

Deficiencies in certain micronutrients can impair your body's ability to protect and heal itself. However, taking vitamins, minerals, and herbs alone will not make up for an unhealthy diet. You still need to eat a healthy diet of fresh vegetables, fruits, and healthy proteins. But supplements are a good safeguard against vitamin and mineral shortfalls in your diet and can help rebuild reduced levels of naturally occurring hormones, such as testosterone.

It's important to consider your overall health as you age. Older men tend to fall into routines that can include eating the same foods over and over again. A repetitive diet often leads to nutrient and micronutrient deficiencies. Dietary supplements can reduce health risks and extend your years of healthy living along with keeping your sex life vibrant.

Red Light Therapy to Boost Your Overall Health

By emitting red, low-light wavelengths through the skin, red light therapy helps naturally jump-start the process of tissue recovery and other forms of rejuvenation through increased blood flow, collagen stimulation, and more. Clinical studies show that red light therapies have certain healing capabilities thanks to the way they positively affect the human endocrine and immune systems.

Although the light is directed at the skin, the light waves cannot be felt and the process isn't painful because it doesn't produce any heat. Red light can be absorbed into the skin to a depth of about 8-to 10 millimeters, at which point it has positive effects on cellular energy and multiple nervous system and metabolic processes.

Red light therapy is used to treat symptoms of joint pain or osteoarthritis due to aging, side effects caused by cancer treatments like chemotherapy or radiation, hair loss, wounds or incisions, acne, wrinkles and skin discoloration, chronic muscular pain, neurological damage, and tissue damage resulting from tears, sprains, or pulls.

A 2012 report published in *Annals in Biomedical Engineering* stated that red light is used in three primary ways: *"to reduce inflammation, edema, and chronic joint disorders; to promote healing of wounds, deeper tissues, and nerves; and to treat neurological disorders and pain."*

It's been found that red light therapy promotes immunity and longevity by increasing cell proliferation and migration, as well as modulating levels of cytokines, growth factors, and inflammatory mediators.

Red light fights estrogen, and estrogen is bad for you in many ways, including aging. Estrogen, when it is not opposed by a very large concentration of progesterone, establishes all of the conditions known to be involved in the aging process.

These include interference with oxidative metabolism, formation of lipofuscin (the age pigment), retention of iron, production of free radicals and lipid peroxides, promotion of excitotoxicity and death of nerve cells, impaired learning ability, increased tendency to form blood clots and to have vascular spasms, increased autoimmunity, atrophy of the thymus, elevated prolactin, atrophy of skin, increased vulnerability to many cancers, lowered body temperature, lower

241

serum albumin, increased tendency toward edema, and untold other symptoms.

That list alone should convince you of the benefits of red light therapy. It also probably sounds like a lot of scientific jargon and you might have trouble understanding it. But take a moment to think back about what you have already learned here about the causes of aging and modern medical problems.

Many of them are closely linked to excess estrogen in your body. Many men have as much estrogen (the so-called female hormone) as women, especially when they are tired or sick. Estrogen increases the brain's susceptibility to epileptic seizures, and recent research shows that it (as well as cortisol) promotes the effects of the excitotoxins, which are increasingly implicated in degenerative brain diseases.

Dr. Ray Peat said in his article "Not the 'female hormone', but the shock hormone:"

> *'While I was studying the effects of light on health, many of the women with the pre- or peri-menstrual syndrome told me that they had few symptoms during the summer months, so I began in the 1960s to examine the role of progesterone in health, because its synthesis is promoted by long days. I saw that many of the sicknesses that mainly*

affect women had often been described as the consequence of an excess of estrogen."

He added:

'1 have concentrated on thyroid, progesterone, and red light as the most important factors that protect against estrogen, and these all turn out to be protective against stress, shock, ionizing radiation, free radicals, lipid peroxidation, thymic atrophy, osteoporosis, arthritis, scleroderma, apoptotic cell death, and other problems that are involved in tissue degeneration or aging."

There is an ever-growing number of studies that have been conducted on the uses of light therapy. Presently, over 2,500 studies and a multitude of articles on the subject have proven its usefulness. Some of the research is specific, such as how light therapy affects diabetic patients or how it can be used in sports medicine to treat tendinopathy. Other studies look at its effects as a treatment for aging, fractures, depression, or as a component of cancer treatment.

Raising Your Oxygen Levels is Among the Most Important Things You Can Do

It seems to go against logic, but 99% of people breathe too much. It doesn't sound intuitive, but breathing too much lowers oxygen levels in organs and tissues. One of the most common symptoms of an anxiety attack is hyperventilation, and hyperventilation is deep, rapid breathing.

Breathing too much affects your whole body. It causes intestinal inflammation, prostate problems, heart problems, even anxiety and depression.

Your blood can be fully saturated with oxygen when you over-breathe, but your organs and tissues will not receive enough oxygen to keep them and your entire body healthy. The reason is the missing CO_2.

The medical term for low CO_2 levels in the blood is hypocapnia.

CO_2 is critical to your body's ability to dilate your blood vessels. Without enough CO_2, **your blood vessels contract and deliver less blood to your organs and tissues.** Less blood being circulated means less oxygen is getting to those organs and tissues. It's the lack of oxygen that causes symptoms.

Hypocapnia creates serious physiological crises throughout your body — it brings on all kinds of physical and mental consequences.

Carbon dioxide helps dilate smooth muscle tissue, including blood vessels. Low carbon dioxide levels can cause spasms throughout the body, including in the brain, bronchi, and other smooth muscle tissues. Asthma and migraines are examples of these spasms.

CO_2 regulates your cardiovascular system, and angina, high blood pressure, chest pain, myocardial infarction (heart attack), strokes, and other serious medical conditions can result from low levels.

CO_2 helps regulate your metabolism. High metabolism rates in cells and tissues generate higher levels of CO_2. The higher levels of CO_2 relaxes (increases diameter) the blood vessels in the immediate area to allow more oxygenation of the tissue and cells experiencing a high metabolic rate.

Other areas of the body with a lower rate of metabolism generate less CO_2.

The result is constriction of the blood vessels and less blood (and oxygen) in the immediate area not in need. This is called tissue hypoxia. Low carbon dioxide brings low oxygen levels and the tissues are dying because they don't have enough oxygen.

It's been shown that as little as one minute of hyperventilation results in 40% less oxygen being available for brain activity.

It's been proven time and again that when ill people begin breathing properly, their CO_2 levels become normal and symptoms decrease almost immediately. Many people report that all symptoms disappear within a few weeks or months.

The correct CO_2 level in your blood is 40 mm Hg CO_2 (a measure of how much pressure is being created by CO_2). This number was established over a century ago by the famous British physiologists Charles G. Douglas and John S. Haldane of Oxford University. Their results were published in 1909 in the article "The regulation of normal breathing" in the *Journal of Physiology*.

Breathing too much causes your arteries to contract, which causes your body organs to receive less oxygen. If you want to learn all of the details about this subject, I have put together several courses on the subject. You can reach me at **matt@getrapidhelp.com**.

There are literally hundreds of disease symptoms that can be overcome simply by correcting your breathing. Breathing affects everything that goes on in your body.

First and foremost, make sure you are breathing through your nose and not your mouth. If you are breathing through your mouth, you almost certainly have health problems.

You even want to nose breathe when you are exercising. If you breathe through your mouth during exercise, you're exerting yourself too much. Back off the level of exertion to a point where can breathe through your nose and then slowly work back up to a higher level of exercise. If you are breathing through your mouth while running, dial it back down to walking until you can run while breathing only through your nose.

The goal of breathing correctly is to gradually reset or readjust your breathing center to higher CO_2 values and reduced minute ventilation (the volume of air breathed). Both parameters, as a result of practiced breathing, should be closer to their norms.

What Your Control Pause Tells You

Your control pause is how long you can comfortably go without taking a breath. Through clinical trials, scientists have reached the following conclusions about the length of control pauses and what they indicate (these are approximate and do not apply to everyone):

❖ 1-5 seconds: severely sick and critically ill patients, usually hospitalized.

❖ 5-10 seconds: very sick patients, often hospitalized.

❖ 10-20 seconds: sick patients with numerous complaints and often on daily medication.

❖ 20-30 seconds: people with poor health but often without serious organic problems.

❖ 30-40 seconds: people with normal health, according to official medical standards, while some serious, often undetected health problems are possible (gastrointestinal, hormonal, and skin problems, caries, intestinal parasites, etc.).

❖ 40-60 seconds: good health.

❖ Over 60 seconds: ideal health, when any organic or other pathological health conditions are virtually impossible.

Avoid Exercise That Harms You

Yes, you need exercise but you need exercise that benefits you, not exercise that harms you. For most people, just having an active lifestyle is all that is needed. Get up and get walking. Use a standing work desk. Take up activities like gardening that require plenty of movement. Active means doing things that stretch your muscles and gets your blood moving.

The so-called **anaerobic** exercise is really aerobic exercise for most people in the beginning, because their lives have become so sedentary.

Usually when we think about exercise, we think of aerobic exercise. That is in part because of the high-energy classes taught at most gyms. However, aerobic exercise is not confined to those classes. For most people, low to moderate exercise or exertion actually is aerobic because they get so little exercise.

So what is the difference between aerobic and **anaerobic** exercise? In the simplest terms, the difference comes down to oxygen.

The words are really used wrong. Aerobic exercise includes running and dancing and swimming. It actually puts your body into a constant state of low oxygen and stress.

Aerobic exercise is continuous activity performed for 15 minutes or longer, resulting in constant stimulation of between 60% and 80% of your maximum heart rate. The longer you exercise, the higher your heart rate. This type of training recruits your slow-twitch muscle fibers and creates lactic acid in your muscles and is really LOW oxygen, so it should be called ANerobic, but it is not.

What they call anaerobic exercise helps build lean muscle mass. Calories are burned more efficiently in bodies that have more muscle (high metabolism). **Anaerobic** exercise is especially helpful for weight management, because it helps to burn more calories even in a body at rest. **Anaerobic** exercise also helps build endurance and fitness levels.

Anaerobic exercise is high-intensity exercise, or exercise at your maximum level of exertion, for short periods of time. Examples include sprinting and weight lifting. To improve their conditioning, athletes use short, high-intensity bursts of anaerobic activity (such as sprints or interval training) followed by longer recovery periods.

Anerobic exercise is much less stressful on the body because the duration is so short. And because it is very intense but short duration, oxygen can reach all the tissues.

To put some numbers on it, the burst of exercise is performed at 80% to 100% of your maximum heart rate, typically for ten to sixty seconds, followed by recovery periods that last three to four times as long as the burst of energy.

There are several benefits to brief intense exercise, such as helping you burn fat faster, but that's not the only reason to work them. "The idea is simple: less total time required to make a big change along with more bang for your buck," says Brent C. Ruby, PhD, FACSM, Director of the Montana Center for Work Physiology and Exercise Metabolism at the University of Montana.

The benefits go far beyond saving time while you get your results — years of research prove it.

Many people find brief intense exercise more enjoyable than low intensity longer session exercise. In fact, one study found that in addition to preferring brief intense exercise over low-intensity but longer exercise sessions, people enjoyed it more than continuous vigorous-intensity exercise and continuous moderate-intensity exercise. The more you enjoy a workout, the more likely you are to stick with it.

Your overall health improves, as can be seen in measurements that show higher counts of mitochondria, which help fuel your body and brain, and improved blood pressure. Brief intense exercise can also lower glucose levels in diabetics, even with a single session.

Another study found that sedentary men, who did forty to sixty minutes of cycling at 65% of their max, five times a week, saw results similar to those who did sprint interval training for less than twelve minutes at a pop, three times a week. Some of those results included reduced aortic stiffness and increased insulin sensitivity.

Brief intense exercise improves the flexibility and elasticity of arteries and veins more effectively than continuous aerobic exercise. Because of the increased pressure demand, the vessels actually get a workout as well. One study that looked at people with coronary artery disease found that brief-intensity interval training was not only safe, but better tolerated than a more moderate-level workout.

You may be surprised to learn that tennis, basketball, racquetball, soccer, volleyball, football, and other start-and-stop sports are anaerobic. This is because when you play those sports, you perform at high heart rates for short durations between longer recovery periods.

Lengthy exercise sessions causes harm. Basically, anything is better than sitting on the couch. But how much exercise is enough and how much is too much?

A 2015 report published in the *Journal of the American College of Cardiology* says that Danish researchers found that people who push their bodies too hard may essentially undo the benefits of the exercise. Those who ran at a fast pace more than four hours a week, for more than three days a week, had about the same risk of dying during the study's twelve-year follow-up as those who were sedentary and hardly exercised at all. Both too little and too much exercise are linked to higher rates of death.

The amount that's just right to maintain heart health, burn off excess calories, and keep blood sugar levels under control is somewhere in between. And according to the study results, that sweet spot is closer to the "less" side of the curve than the "more" side.

This agrees with a mounting body of recent research that's finding that so-called micro-workouts (high-intensity but brief workouts that could be as short as one minute) may be better for the body than long and continuous workouts.

Exercising excessively or incorrectly can backfire on you and your health in a number of ways. Here are some of the things that could result from exercising too much or too hard:

❖ Your immune system may be weakened.

❖ Your body could enter a catabolic state resulting in your tissues breaking down.

❖ Excess cortisol (a stress hormone) could be released. This not only contributes not only to catabolism, but also to chronic disease, **including intestinal inflammation.**

❖ You could develop microscopic tears in your muscle fibers (which may fail to heal if you continue over-exercising) and increase your risk for injuries.

❖ You may begin to suffer from insomnia, especially if your workout is in the afternoon or evening.

However, the most serious risk involves damaging your heart or, worse still, **sudden cardiac death.** The results of several recent scientific studies indicate that endurance exercises, such as marathon and triathlon training, pose significant risks to your heart, some of which may be irreversible and life-threatening. Long-distance running can lead to acute volume overload, inflammation, thickening and stiffening of the heart muscle and arteries, coronary artery calcification, arrhythmias, and sudden cardiac arrest.

Growth Hormone Ages You — Not Good

Call it anti-anti-aging therapy. It turns out that injections of growth hormone — a staple of anti-aging, hormone-replacement therapy — has the opposite effect from that intended, actually thwarting a person's quest to live to an advanced age.

In an ongoing study of very old people, those in their 90s with naturally low levels of human growth hormone appear to have a far better chance of living into their 100s than people with above average levels of the hormone.

In other words, taking growth hormones as an anti-aging strategy will almost certainly backfire, as it will actually undermine the body's natural defenses against the diseases of old age, according to researchers at Albert Einstein College of Medicine in New York. Their study appears in the April 2014 issue of the journal *Aging Cell*.

The billion-dollar anti-aging hormone-therapy industry is based on a simple premise: Levels of a variety of hormones decrease significantly as adults hit middle age. Therefore, replenishing those hormones to youthful levels should make graying adults look and feel younger. The primary hormones administered by anti-aging clinics are human growth hormones (HGH), which prompt the body to make insulin-like growth factor 1 (IGF-1) and dehydroepiandrosterone (DHEA), a precursor of estrogen and testosterone.

This industry traces its roots to a 1990 *New England Journal of Medicine* study, in which 12 men over the age of 60 were given shots of growth hormone. The men experienced a modest increase in muscle mass and bone density, and a decline in body fat. To some entrepreneurs, that meant "anti-aging," and they have repackaged the study that way ever since.

But the treatment comes with side effects and a myriad of unknowns. The study's author, Dr. Daniel Rudman, remained resolute until his death that his study had no implications for anti-aging.

Prescribing HGH is illegal unless the patient has low levels of the hormone. However, the diagnosis is subjective, enabling some clinics to prescribe the treatment to people who don't actually fit the intended profile and can be harmed by it — but can afford it.

Studies have since shown that using HGH, estrogen, and other hormones as treatments can lead to cancer, cardiovascular disease, joint problems, and other ailments.

In a new study, researchers followed 184 men and women in their mid-90s for up to 11 years. Strikingly, the chance of living through the duration of the study depended mostly on the participants' blood levels of IGF-1 (insulin-like Growth Factor-1). Each nanogram per milliliter fewer of IGF-1 translated into about one more week of life.

The lower IGF-1 levels were particularly beneficial for cancer survivors. Three years after entering the study, 75% of participants with low IGF-1 levels who had previously had cancer were still living. However, only about 25% of participants with higher IGF-1 levels who had previously had cancer were alive.

'In light of insufficient scientific evidence [that] HGH in older adults offers long-term anti-aging benefits, and with studies indicating that low growth hormone levels may actually protect the elderly from aging diseases... the risks of using HGH as an anti-

aging strategy outweigh the potential benefits," said Dr. Sofiya Milman, lead author of the new study and an assistant professor of endocrinology at Albert Einstein College of Medicine.

Enough said... HGH is NOT the fountain of youth!

Be Continuously Active

That means **stop being a couch potato.** Parking on the couch often begins in adolescence, when young people watch hours of TV, eat more junk food, exercise less, study less, have fewer friends, and are more likely to be involved in drugs and alcohol. Adults who watch lots of TV are more likely to be overweight, depressed, have cardiovascular diseases, and live shorter lives. Wow!

If you're not ready to start a regular exercise routine, at least start moving around more. If you're lethargic and unmotivated, **CHANGE SOMETHING, CHANGE ANYTHING!** Begin around the house.

It's not just that we don't get enough exercise. We've become an inactive society. A few short generations ago, our ancestors did plenty of physical labor and didn't need to make time to exercise regularly. They worked on farms, did manual labor in factories, or dug ditches by hand. Nothing was automated.

Today, when broad studies are done about how much physical activity people are getting, these studies include the few steps that it takes you to walk to your car to drive to the store as a physical activity. We use remote controls for everything. As couch potatoes, we don't even get up to change the TV channel any more. Our ovens are self-cleaning and there are robot vacuum cleaners. Little wonder we've become an obese society.

Do your chores. Stop using the dishwasher — wash the dishes yourself. Save a few bucks by not using a lawn service — mowing the lawn and gardening are great exercise. Buy some five-pound dumbbells to at least start doing light exercise during TV commercials. **DO SOMETHING.**

Nick Turns His Health Around

This is a composite story developed from the stories of multiple students. All student identities are fully protected at all times. Any similarity to any actual person is completely coincidental.

Nick lived a life that was typical of many men he knew. He thought it was a healthy modern life. However, at age 48 and as a married man, he was becoming concerned about his health. His doctor had recently put him on high blood pressure medicine and warned him to cut back on sugars because he was dangerously close to developing type 2 diabetes.

The kids were grown and gone. He and his wife thought they were eating a healthy diet of mostly vegetables, chicken, and fish. However, the "healthy" foods they were eating were actually processed foods like breaded frozen fish, chicken nuggets, and canned vegetables. They would splurge by having a pizza about once a week, and during the summer Nick liked to BBQ a thick steak occasionally.

At age 48, Nick and his wife worked hard but didn't really play hard. Financially, they were in good shape, but instead of being active by traveling or getting out into nature, they tended to be couch potatoes. She read a lot and he watched a lot of old westerns. Yep, over the years, both of them put on about thirty extra pounds that slowed them down even more.

All of this had brought their sex life to a standstill — no sex drive and no erections for Nick.

Nick thinks about growing older. Despite thinking he was living a healthy modern life, his medical diagnoses and his weight gain did begin to cause him some anxiety. Nick began to realize that maybe he wasn't so healthy. He had been told repeatedly that the processed foods he'd been eating for decades weren't good for him. However, he thought his work schedule made it impractical for him to cook healthy meals every day.

Nick began doing some research into what might constitute a healthy diet. This was very recently, and he became confused when he found conflicting information: some told him to eat less fat and more carbohydrates, and newer information said he should cut back on the carbs and eat more protein and healthy fats. But, one thing that was strongly recommended no matter what advice he read was that he should eat fresh, wholesome food and not processed foods.

Nick decided that if he wanted to get healthier and live to an old age, it was time for him to change his diet. He and his wife began doing most of their own cooking. The new diet they took up was the popular high-fat and low-carbohydrates diet.

Nick didn't even bother talking about it with his doctor before making the diet change. He was sure the diet change would lower his risk of developing type 2 diabetes. After about six months on the new diet, Nick went in for his semiannual medical checkup. **To his complete surprise, he had gained another four pounds and the doctor wanted to put him on a low dosage of diabetic medicine.**

Nick talks to his doctor. This is when Nick started a conversation with his doctor about how confused he was about the different diet information he had found in his research. The doctor told him that he really didn't stay current with nutrition information, but he thought the diet Nick was eating and the medicines he had prescribed would keep him healthy enough to keep working until his retirement years.

The doctor also told Nick that if he wanted more information about diets, he should talk to a nutritionist or a dietitian. He gave Nick a couple of recommendations.

Nick did follow up with a nutritionist about a week later and again explained his confusion and how his health had actually deteriorated on the high-fat and low-carbohydrate diet. The nutritionist wasn't surprised. She said that a lot of clinical studies over the past ten years have shown that a low-carbohydrate diet was a recipe for poor health and a no-fat diet caused nutrient deficiency.

She also said that most professionals who specialized in this area were well aware of the changes in recommended diets but the word wasn't getting out to other medical professionals. The medical profession has become so specialized that none of them can keep up with all of the changes. For instance, his diabetic specialist probably did everything that he can to stay current with all of the new diabetic medicines coming on the market.

The nutritionist gave Nick a diet plan that closely resembled the one recommended to overcome intestinal inflammation. She also told him to check back with her and his diabetic specialist in about six weeks. She thought his diabetic specialist would want to downward adjust or even take him off the medicine. She also recommended that he check in with a high blood pressure doctor at about the same time.

Nick recovers his health. Nick continued researching healthy diets and finally came upon Matt Cook's Advanced ED Cure, and hence, the anti-inflammation diet. Nick and his wife have been closely following that diet ever since. He quickly concluded that making time to cook his own fresh food was essential to his health as he aged. And of course, everyone knows that if you don't have your health, you don't have anything.

Nick and his wife have been on their new healthy diet for about two months now. However, it took several weeks for them to source some of the fresh foods. The grass fed-beef wasn't difficult to find, but they had to search around for a butcher that sold grass-fed lamb and goat from New Zealand. They also found a specialty store that featured grass-fed butter, other grass-fed dairy products, and eggs from free-range chickens.

Although they started their new diet a couple of months ago, in reality it took a while for them to find all of the right foods that they wanted to eat. That means it will probably be another month or so before they have full relief from gut inflammation and reap the other benefits of a good old-fashioned diet.

Their sex drive has returned with vigor. Both of them regained their sex drive pretty quickly. Today, Nick often wakes up with morning wood, but it will probably be another month or so before he can achieve an erection every time he and his wife become romantic.

However, they are engaging in **Oxytocin Behaviors.** They cuddle naked almost every morning and are sure to include other oxytocin behaviors throughout the day. When Nick doesn't achieve an erection during the naked cuddling, they often use the soft entry method. Overall, they feel much healthier, have a much healthier sex life, and have only the positive to look forward to as they grow older.

How to Raise Your T and Lower Estrogen

As already established, men need some estrogen. Just not nearly as much as most modern men have. The biggest problem is that estrogen in men is created from our precious testosterone. The conversion takes place via an enzyme called aromatase.

As men age, the rate of this conversion becomes more pronounced. But if you take action, you can dial that back and maintain high levels of T.

Let's begin with some specific and unfortunate

effects that too much estrogen can have on the male body:

❖ Enlarged breasts on men.

❖ Erectile dysfunction.

❖ Loss of confidence.

❖ Higher voice.

❖ Loss of body hair.

❖ Decrease in muscle mass.

❖ Increase in fatty tissue.

❖ Prostate enlargement.

❖ Lower sex drive.

❖ Difficulty losing weight.

All of those are the opposite of what high or even mid-range testosterone levels will do. Too much estrogen will turn you into a man-woman.

All estrogen is not the same. There are three types of estrogen. You should become familiar with each of them.

❖ **Estrone (E1).** This is a weaker estrogen found in post-menopausal women.

❖ **Estradiol (E2).** This is the strongest estrogen.

Normally, men have about half as much as women. Its primary role in men is to extend the life of sperm to increase the chance of pregnancy from intercourse. This is the type that male testes convert from testosterone — T aromatizes into estradiol.

A similar conversion also takes place in the brain where it influences feelings and behaviors. The aromatase enzyme is necessary to convert T to E. You also need it for your T and E to be in balance.

❖ **Estriol (E3).** This is the type of estrogen that's dominant in pregnant women.

How Much Estrogen Should You Have? The reality is that younger men have more testosterone than most older guys. The T to E ratio can be as high as 50:1 in young men, but the more common ratio is around 40:1. Older men who have let themselves go will have a low ratio, down around 7:1. These are the men with a spare tire and/or type 2 diabetes. Just by putting some of the lifestyle guidance from this book into practice you can quickly double the ratio to about 15:1.

The most important key to obtaining and maintaining a healthy T to E ratio is by removing estrogen and estrogen-converting contaminates from your food and skin. The next section of this book is going to shock you, because you're going to find out how prevalent estrogen is in our modern world.

Why Modern Men Have Elevated E

❖ **Obesity:** Studies have shown that obesity is directly related to elevated estrogen levels. All fat cells contain the aromatase enzyme. The more aromatase you have, the more estrogen you will have.

❖ **Zinc deficiency:** Zinc inhibits aromatase. Without adequate zinc, your aromatase levels rise. Diuretics are used to treat several medical conditions including high blood pressure, heart failure, and hypertension. Diuretics also lower zinc levels in the body. Taking a zinc supplement can return zinc levels to the correct level.

❖ **Poor liver function:** An important function of the liver is the elimination of chemicals, hormones, drugs, and metabolic waste products from your body. A poorly-functioning liver can cause all kinds of problems.

❖ **Alcohol:** Besides interfering with your liver function, consuming alcohol leads directly to increases of estrogen in the blood. Heavy drinkers will have elevated estrogen levels.

❖ **Prescription medicines:** Some medicines will, as a side effect, directly or indirectly cause a rise in estrogen. Diuretics are used to treat several medical conditions including high blood pressure, heart failure, and hypertension. Diuretics also lower zinc levels in the body. Taking a zinc supplement can return zinc levels to the correct level.

Environmental estrogen is a major problem with our food supply, but it's not getting much media attention. Our food supply is seriously contaminated with many forms of estrogen. It wasn't like this fifty or sixty years ago. But with big corporations managing our food chain, they have completely polluted it in favor of cheap profits.

Where is it? It's in the hormone injections that our meats are given and the food they are force-fed. It's in the billions of tons of pesticides in grains that are grown on mechanical farms. There probably is not a safe loaf of bread on any grocery shelf in the country.

In the food supply, there are many types of **pseudo-estrogens** that kill your testosterone levels. They have different names but probably **the worst is xenoestrogen.** Sorry to say, this baddie is found throughout the food chain. It's in:

❖ Commercially-raised, non-organic beef, chicken,

pork, and other meats, and farmed fish.

❖ Soy beans, tofu, soy beverages, and soy oil (soy sauce is okay).

❖ Cottonseed oil (widely used in processed foods and as animal food).

❖ Hops in beer (both alcoholic and non-alcoholic).

❖ Red clover in supplement form.

❖ Queen Anne's lace (wild carrot).

❖ Pomegranate — the Greeks used this plant as a contraceptive! That's how badly it affects your sex life.

❖ Dates

❖ Coffee

❖ Fennel

❖ Licorice

❖ Motherwort

❖ Bloodroot

❖ Ocotillo

❖ Alfalfa sprouts

❖ Sunflower seeds

❖ Mandrake

❖ Oregano

❖ Damiana

❖ Pennyroyal

❖ Verbena

❖ Nutmeg

❖ Turmeric

❖ Yucca

❖ Thyme

- ❖ Calamus root
- ❖ Cumin
- ❖ Goldenseal
- ❖ Chamomile
- ❖ Mistletoe
- ❖ Cloves

Plastics, microwaves, and household products turn you into a man-woman. Plastics release very bad chemicals into your body. NEVER EVER microwave food in plastic containers and don't even store food in plastic. This includes water bottles. Also, avoid Teflon cookware. Teflon is pure poison. Use ceramic cookware. Stainless steel can be okay, but ceramic is better.

Shampoos and detergents are on the list too. For shampooing and washing, I suggest Dr. Bronner's unscented baby soap. You can also use this for washing dishes and cleaning the house (such as floors).

A 2011 study published in *Environmental Health Perspectives* found that 70% of manufactured plastics contain compounds that have estrogenic activity. More importantly, **the number skyrocketed to 95%** when plastics were subjected to everyday activities like microwaving and dishwashing.

Exposure to estrogen-active plastics is known to alter the structure of human cells.

Phthalates are a group of chemical compounds used

to make plastics softer and more resistant to breaking. They are also used as lubricants in cosmetics. These are found in thousands of everyday household items, from drink containers to hairspray to deodorant to toys. More than a billion pounds of phthalates compounds are manufactured in the US every year. But you won't find them on any ingredient list.

Also, avoid phytoestrogens. These are in food products containing soy, quercetin, resveratrol, and alcohol. Some of those products may have some benefits, but those benefits are far outweighed by the estrogens they bring into your body.

If you want an occasional beer, go with the blonde beers. Stay away from the IPAs and dark beers. In general, all alcohol is loaded with estrogens. That's why men that are heavy or even moderate drinkers tend to have sexual dysfunction problems.

Modern meat is for women. Estrogen is so prevalent in commercially grown meat that men should probably be prohibited from eating it. Of course, we don't want to take men's rights away to that extent... but, I'm just saying.

How do you think farmed salmon gets to be ready for market twice as fast as wild salmon? They're stuffed with hormones, of course. Estrogen-fed cattle gain 20% more weight than grass-fed cattle do. And dairy cows on estrogen produce 15%

more milk. Do you ever wonder exactly what's in that extra 15% of milk or extra 20% of fattened beef?

All of the ways that estrogen, other hormones, and pesticides are used in commercial food production would take an entire book to describe and would be outdated at the moment of publishing because of all the creative ways corporations come up with to artificially increase and speed up production.

Little testing has been conducted on how hormone-infused meat affects humans. From the few studies that have been done, it's known that certain hormones lower the sperm count in men. Europe has banned artificial hormones in beef for years and in 1989 banned the import of U.S. beef. Canada, Japan, Australia, and other countries have also banned certain hormones from being used in the meat industry.

More than a decade ago, the National Cancer Institute warned of the carcinogenic risks posed by estrogenic additives, which can cause imbalances and increases in natural hormone levels. Currently, there is no hormone residue testing in the cattle industry. Synthetic hormones closely resemble naturally-occurring hormones. Yet the use of these artificial hormones is completely unregulated.

If you are a meat eater, your option is eating organic meat only. Or you can talk to your butcher about the availability of hormone-free meat.

But let's end on a much more positive note...

You Have Whole-Body O's This Way

Enjoy hours of whole-body orgasmic waves of sexual bliss every day. This works for guys that have had ED for years, marital sex that has gone dead in the bedroom, and men that haven't been with a woman for years.

DON'T LET SEX FADE AWAY FROM YOUR LIFE

This is about extreme sexual pleasure by overcoming desensitization. If you have a porn or masturbation addiction, you'll immediately overcome it. You'll become enthralled with your woman again. It all has to do with becoming more and more sexually sensitive.

It's about having full body O's... and you NEVER get that "spent" feeling of tiredness and that "I can't possibly do it again" feeling...

Each time you're intimate, she's loving it more and more.

Since I learned how to have whole-body O's, I don't need to be thrusting away for us to feel pleasure. I still love to thrust, but now we: change speeds, stop, kiss, tease, and whatever else feels good.

And I achieve whole-body O's... it's just so crazy.

Last night, we were really tired, but we lay down for a little bit of fun, and wow! I was just going from one mind-blowing O to the next. It was crazy.

Shortly after it began, SHE begged me to teach her.

Imagine, my wife asking me how to do whole-body O's.

For you, as you grow older, instead of becoming less and less sensitive to sexual pleasure, you can completely reverse that. It will become 100x, 500x, 1,000x more pleasurable for both you and her. You will become more and more sensitive to sex — forever! Intercourse goes on for half an hour, an hour, and longer while you experience multiple whole-body orgasms. That's waves of orgasmic pleasure!

You'll never again feel that you're not getting enough sex. Instead, you'll forever anticipate sex becoming better and better for both of you as time goes on. **Well into your 80s, 90s, and beyond.**

Bring on the Oxytocin

Everything we've gone over so far is important. However, **none of it is as important as this part.** Dopamine is the chemical in your brain that tells you to pursue something that creates pleasure for you. When it comes to dating, it's dopamine that tells you to have sex with her. It's what heats the relationship up for both of you.

The problem with dopamine sex is that it is over way too fast. For some, it can be over in four minutes or less. For most, it's over in ten minutes or less. This is hot, fast sex based on the two of you stimulating each other to a rapid orgasm.

As you probably know, most women take longer than men to climax but, once the man climaxes, it's over for both of them — for several hours or days at least. That leaves a lot to be desired when it comes to dopamine-based sex.

A much better way of becoming sexually aroused is upping the amount of oxytocin in your brain. This takes some time and requires some behavior changes on your part, but, for the effort, you will have much better and much longer sex sessions. You'll be able to stay hard and inside of her for a half hour or longer. It will be a profound change in your lovemaking. It will send her over the top again and again. You won't be able to get enough of her and she won't be able to get enough of you. But you'll both be getting more of each other than you ever have before.

What makes this even more powerful is that it creates incredible levels of intimacy. Oxytocin lovemaking involves much more physical contact than you've ever had with a woman before. It creates a mental- and soul-bonding that you absolutely must experience. The same will happen with her. The two of you will become lifetime lovers. That is the reason it so important to be with the right woman before becoming involved with oxytocin lovemaking.

Explaining to Her That You Don't Want Sex Right Away

Building up oxytocin takes a little time, but it's certainly worth it. You have to refrain from having sex for two or three weeks. During that time, you do lots of cuddling, especially naked cuddling. About a half hour of naked cuddling each day. The two of you are in a new type of relationship, so this is going to take some commitment on both of your parts. But the magic of oxytocin lovemaking is certainly worth it.

While dopamine sex is about stimulating each other to a fast orgasm, oxytocin lovemaking is about sensation. You can enjoy sensations much longer than stimulation sex. That's why oxytocin leads to very long sex sessions.

Women love to be chased, and this is a great way of creating a chase. When you postpone sex, she'll want to know where she stands with her man.

Tell her up front that you want to make this very

special for both of you. That you want to drive your desire for each other to the peak before making love. That you want to do a lot of kissing and hand holding and cuddling on the couch. That you desire her body and want to get naked in bed, but the next two weeks are dedicated to building up oxytocin and strong, strong desires for each other.

Tell her," I love sex a lot and want to have great sex with you because I think you're super-hot." This will motivate her to stick around to discover what is coming next.

If she just wants to get down and do the deed, she probably isn't the woman for you. You're showing resolve that you can do what you want and what is best for both of you. A real woman will understand this and see you for the man that you are. You are showing that you value her. Women love and need this kind of attention from men.

She will get hot to have sex. When she initiates a sexual act, remind her that you think she is hot, and for THAT REASON you and she are waiting a bit.

Women very, very much like kissing. It's a huge sexual turn on for her. Put your full effort into kissing her during the buildup to oxytocin sex. Kiss her often and for no apparent reason. Kiss her in all of her sensual places. The back of the neck, behind her ears, her wrist, her elbow, her feet, and her legs. She'll be begging you for sex, but you're going to do this for two or three weeks.

The longer you wait the better the reward!

The other thing you want to do is stroke her often and in many different parts of her body. This is an extremely light stroke. So light that it feels to her more like a light breeze flowing over her skin. Ask her where she wants to be stroked, but you can start with her lower back, her neck and shoulders, her wrists, and, teasingly, her legs and thighs.

Don't make this stroking too sexual. Keep it at a level that doesn't lead to sex. Or, if you're getting close to having intercourse back off for a moment. This is all about the buildup of sensations rather than stimulating the two of you.

Now for Slow Passionate Sex

You're ready for sex when you start having spontaneous erections. You get hard when you see her or think about her. When you decide to have sex, you should naturally be hard. Don't have her manually or orally stimulate you unless you are already hard.

Sometime before having sex, you need to explain the orgasm scale that goes from 1 (nothing sexual) to 10 (orgasm). **You want to enter her slowly and just leave your penis there. Feel the sensations and let her feel the sensations. This type of sex requires very little movement.**

On the orgasm scale you want to stay around 5, 6, or 7. If you edge up to 8 or 9, it's time to slow things down so that you can stay with the sensations instead of the stimulation.

She's allowed to orgasm, because women are more capable of multiple orgasms than men. She should experience several orgasms during your half hour of sex. Men have multiple orgasms too, but these are different from the intense orgasms that women have.

You should experience periods when you are having several small orgasms. These should NOT make you ejaculate. That's why you can stay hard inside of her for much, much longer than with stimulation sex.

During these long sex sessions, tell her what you are doing to her and tell her what you want her to do to you. You'll find this heightens the sensations even further.

TRY IT, YOU'LL LOVE IT, BOTH OF YOU'LL NEVER GET ENOUGH OF IT!!